HOW TO PLAN YOUR DIY WEDDING

Your step-by-step guide to building a personalised and meaningful wedding.

LAURA STROUD

Randan Press

How to Plan Your DIY Wedding

Copyright © 2021 Laura Stroud

ISBN – Paperback: 978-1-913911-18-8

Published by Randan Press.

Disclaimer:

This book is a work of non-fiction based on the author's research into the subject matter. Although the author has made every effort to ensure the information in this book was correct at the time of press, the author does not assume and hereby disclaims any liability to any party for any loss, damage, or disruption caused by errors or omissions, whether such errors or omissions result from negligence, accident, or any other cause. This is not professional or legal advice; you should seek specific support for your personal situation. The names mentioned in the book have been changed, to protect privacy.

Contents

Congratulations!

Dear Reader,

You are engaged! This is so exciting. I'm really happy for you. You are about to embark on a wonderful and joyous journey. A unique and special time in your life, but you already know that, right?

My wish for you is that in every moment leading up to your wedding day you feel full of energy and excitement. Instead of worry, stress or anxiety. If life works out as planned, we only get married once; we only get this day once in our whole lives. I want yours to be special and memorable. The way to achieve this is simple — hard work, lots of planning and a sprinkle of love.

This book is for you to write in, scribble on, stick ideas to, rip out activities, draw on blank pages and treasure forever. This is a step-by-step practical guide that cuts through some of the basics and delves deep into the details that other books don't cover. You already know you can save money by serving tap water instead of bottled water; you don't need a book to tell you that. However:

- Do you know how to turn a Pinterest idea into a unique wedding favour, without it being a carbon copy?
- Do you know how to prioritise your tasks so the wedding ideas closest to your heart get the most attention?
- Do you know how to make your wedding extra-special?
- Do you know how to make your wedding unique?

Stick with me and I can show you how. I've got years and years of experience working in and on events, especially weddings. I'll share my knowledge, industry secrets and experience in this book to ensure you bring your dream wedding to life. Think of it as having your very own personal wedding planner, dishing out all the advice and tips we wished everyone planning a wedding knew before they started.

Before we even start, I'm going to tell you the biggest secret of all, just so you know it up front. Then we can dive into all of the juicy, delicious details of how to make your day memorable.

The biggest secret: There is no such thing as perfect. The perfect wedding doesn't exist. It's a lie.

There, I said it. I'm sorry. I'm breaking all the rules. But it's important this book is truthful, so you can know from the start that I'm on your side. I'm not going to feed into the lies the wedding industry can whisper.

There is no such thing as the perfect wedding.

But with a little bit of planning, a lot of hard work and heaps of heart you can have something better than the perfect wedding. You can create a *meaningful* wedding, a personal wedding. A wedding that *really* represents you as a couple, a wedding that will tell the stories of your lives and a wedding that people will *still* be talking about for years to come. That's so much better than a carbon copy of a magazine wedding, and it's even better than a perfect wedding.

It's real.

Your wedding will be incredible because it will be true to you and your values. It will showcase the love and life you want to build, it will be more meaningful than perfect. That's what people will remember, and that's what *you'll* remember. That's what will make your wedding different, that's what will make it stand out.

Why you should buy this book:

- Written by a wedding planner and wedding coordinator who specialises in DIY weddings, I'll share the secrets and hints that you would normally have to pay for. You will reap the experience gained from my years of wedding and event planning.
- You will develop confidence in your wedding decisions. There is a clear emphasis on understanding how you want your wedding to 'feel' and why, ensuring that your wedding day is a reflection of your values and wishes.
- You will learn how to create detailed wedding day

plans. These will help you design your wedding and will lead to less stress and more creativity.

- You will learn how to cut through the list of 'should haves' and plan the wedding you *really* want rather than fulfil the expectations of others.

This book is structured to keep the momentum up. It's fast-paced, and jam-packed with tips and ideas that you won't find anywhere else.

And the best part? This book is going to set you up with the practical skills and step-by-step plans to allow you to not only plan a unique and memorable wedding, but you can also use these same tools and skills to create beautiful and meaningful events and parties. The ideas are transferrable. I'm giving you all of my best advice right here in this book. You can take away all of these steps and the advice to plan *any* event, not just a wedding.

Sounds good?

Let's make your wedding memorable and personal. Let's get to work.

Love,

Laura

Book Overview

Part One - Setting the Scene

In this section you will begin to get clear about your desired outcomes and your vision for your wedding day. This means unpicking what *really* matters to you. You might think you have a clear idea in your head, but when you've got family helpfully 'suggesting' ideas, wedding traditions and Pinterest piling the pressure on, things can get a little muddled. Expectations can get in the way, and you can feel like you've started heading down a path you never intended to go down. This part of the book will show you how to put a stop to that.

How will this specifically help you?

Part one will allow you to create a clear vision for your wedding. With a crystal-clear focus, you will be able to communicate your wedding vision and ensure other people understand the ideas behind your big day. Get people on board and put them to work.

Part Two - Exploring Your Options

In part two you will work through the core foundations of your wedding. The who, the what, the where and the "HOW MUCH?!". Once you've got a really good idea of the vision for your wedding, you can look at some of the details in more depth. You will create timelines and look at the order of the wedding day, highlighting what needs to be done and when.

How will this specifically help you?

This section will allow you to complete a timeline for your wedding, the most important and key foundation of the whole process. You will begin to highlight the tasks you need to prioritise, and you will have a clear starting point and definitive direction.

Part Three - Making Plans

In part three you delve into *even more* detailed plans and look at how to develop a working document (don't worry, we will cover what this is). We'll look at delegation packs and task lists. The best thing you can do to create the wedding of your dreams is plan, plan and plan some more. The goal is to plan everything so much it looks like it all just happened. One big coincidence. This is how you'll create a stress-free wedding. I will give you some of the best tips and advice that I've collected from brides and grooms over the years.

This section is going to be hard, because it's all about the details. You will need to put a lot of work into the planning process. But I promise, if you can plan everything with a minute level of detail, you will suddenly reach a point where your wedding doesn't feel planned, it feels *natural*. A wedding like this is free-flowing. You'll hear people make comments such as:

"Oh, isn't it lucky how this has worked out?"

"Wow! That's good that this venue is here."

"What a coincidence!"

"This venue worked so well with all the different spaces, what a lucky find."

Your guests might not realise that everything went to plan because you prepared, because you noticed the details. But you'll know that's why it's all come together.

How will this specifically help you?

This section will allow you to create detailed plans that take away the stress and worry that is caused by being disorganised. Your wedding will be so well planned you could hand it over to a stranger and they would know how to see it through. This helps you feel less stressed and more in control. You really can't over plan.

Part Four - What Happens if it All Goes Wrong?

Lots of wedding planning books don't talk about this. It's much easier to only plan for events to work out rather than even take a quick glance at the possibility of what could go wrong. In this section we look at some of the elements that could go wrong, and what to do to mitigate them. You'll make plans for the unexpected and the crazy. And I'll introduce you to my top-secret wedding planning tool,

'The Doom List'. I use this almost daily in my event management work to plan for problems and solve them before they happen, it has saved me time and time again in all the events and weddings I've managed.

How will this specifically help you?

You will have a step-by-step guide to deal with the most common wedding problems, removing stress as we try and tackle the unknown. You will have solid contingency plans and wedding risk assessments. This section will also allow you to maximise your wedding enjoyment and minimise stress. Who doesn't want that?

Part Five - The Happily Ever After

You're married, *now what?* In this section we will look at the often-forgotten elements that make a wedding, the clearing down, the tidying up and the taboo of the 'wedding blues'. What really happens when your dreams come true? In this section we'll also explore how to document and capture your wedding day for years to come.

How will this specifically help you?

You will have a post-wedding action plan supporting your transition into married life. You'll be prepared to savour some of the elements of your wedding day that so often get lost in the tidy up and closedown.

How to use this book

This book is jam-packed, and it's going to seem really fast-paced as we move through the sections. That's because this allows you to really build momentum. It allows you to consolidate your learning, but it also lets you get to the big picture quickly, allowing you to see what you *really* need to focus on and when.

Each chapter works like a toolkit, with sections broken down to include:

- **Activities** – Step-by-step instructions to help you plan your wedding.
- **Examples** – Ideas from real brides I've worked with and personal stories I share from my own DIY wedding to help inspire and guide you.
- **Tips** – Some extra advice for key moments in your wedding planning journey, often sourced from personal experience or industry standard suggestions.
- **Questions** – This book will ask you to consider questions about your wedding to help you plan with more confidence.
- **Section Summaries** – At the end of each section there is a clear summary of what we've covered. You can tick off the tasks you've completed or the elements you've learnt, and you can see what's coming next.
- **Homework** – At the end of each section there will also be 'homework' tasks. These activities should be completed between each section to help you get the most out of the book. Don't worry, it will be fun homework!

I would recommend working through each chapter and the activities in order, planning and allocating time to work through the tasks, then going back and digging into any chapters you may want to explore further or share with your partner. By working through the tasks, you are going to have all the details of your wedding sorted.

Make sure you have fun at every possible moment! Planning your wedding should be as stress-free as possible.

What you'll need:

- A brand-new sparkling wedding notebook. The prettier the better. Treat yourself to some new stationery so you can feel like working on your wedding is a joy. You can use the notebook to make notes or jot down ideas as you go in the margins of the book.
- Pens and highlighters. Circle, highlight, underline anything in the book that really resonates with you.
- A calendar would be good too. This can be as simple as a printed-out wall chart, or just your diary would be fine. You'll want to start plotting out tasks that need to be completed.

Stick with me and get ready to work hard but have lots of fun in the process! The story of your wedding day will be one that people will be telling for a long time.

Part One – Setting the Scene

ONE

Your Wedding Story

Your wedding should tell a story.

It should be something that people talk about for years to come. It should set you up with wonderful memories and enough stories to last a lifetime. It is so easy to fall into the trap of planning your wedding the same way everyone else does. But the problem with this is that you will get the same results.

A carbon copy wedding.

You want *your* wedding to stand out and be different. You want people to remember *your* wedding, and to do that you need to tell a story

This is how you will make your wedding different from everyone else's. It will completely reflect who you are, your relationship with your partner, and all of the wonderful ideas you've had circling in your head since before you can remember. Let's be honest, you've been dreaming of this for a while.

When you tell a story with your wedding, you are creating a personal and meaningful experience for you and your guests. You are sharing the chapters of your life and reflecting the journey you've been on to reach this point.

What do we mean by stories?

People remember stories. They remember the time they cried when a friend, beautiful inside and out, walked down the aisle after years of trying to find the right partner. Or the story of the friend who had a joyous first dance at their wedding after years of living with anxiety. We remember these stories because they are full of meaning and feeling.

What story do you want to tell with your wedding?

- Do you want people to tell the story of how two people fell in love and their world then changed?
- Or the story of how a community of people supported and nurtured a love that grew into a marriage?
- Or the story of how a single parent found a person to trust and blend a new life with?
- Or the story of how two people falling in love and committing to spend their lives together can make the world stop for a day?
- Or something else? Something completely different?

Stories matter because they are the essence of who we are. People won't remember what your wedding looked like. They will remember the story you told and how it made them *feel*.

Stories from a real wedding

Lucy was one of my DIY brides, I helped coordinate and plan her wedding and I ran the 'show' on the day. Lucy was beautiful (inside and out). She had been planning her wedding for years and years, and she had so many wonderful ideas. Crazy, bold, beautiful ideas and she knew *exactly* what she wanted her wedding to look like, right down to where every candleholder would hang and in which tree.

My worry for Lucy, though, was that she was so focused on how she wanted her wedding to *look*, she forgot about how she wanted it to *feel*. She forgot to think about how she wanted to feel on her wedding day and, in doing this, she was missing out on so much!

She was worried and stressed about where decorations needed to be and how the stairs needed to be dressed, that she snapped at her husband-to-be, she forgot to drink water and she missed the arrival of her friend from overseas. Lucy was so busy *planning* her wedding she wasn't *present* in her wedding. She was missing it. All of the beautiful details, the people, the memories. These special moments were going unnoticed and, more importantly, she wasn't even looking after herself. It's so easy to do. To slip into this mindset. Friends and wedding professionals can nudge and suggest, but ultimately Lucy was telling the story of her wedding through her actions.

It was a story filled with stress, worry and perfection. The story she wanted to tell, the story her friends and family wanted to be a part of, was one of love, creativity and kindness. The message was just getting a little lost in the mess. Rather than embracing support and help, Lucy tried to do everything herself, because she thought she was showing her love and care for others through perfection by creating a perfect wedding.

But Lucy was exhausted, a little run-down and rattled by the time she walked down the aisle. Sure, her day was still incredible, but the story wasn't one she wanted. It wasn't the one she set out to tell. The ideal of perfection and appearance can hinder the real story.

How to tell a story with your wedding

This is where the idea for this book was born. After watching too many brides and grooms miss out on some of the best parts of their wedding, after seeing them exhausted as they walked down the aisle, I knew I needed to help. This book is based around the idea that you need to plan your wedding, of course, but you need to be *present* in it too. You need to understand how you want your wedding to *feel*, not just what it will *look* like and in doing this you'll create the wedding you've always wanted.

I want to help you to see the big picture *and* the details. I want you to enjoy all the parts of your wedding but prioritise the parts that mean the most to you and let the other stuff go. So, you can stand in the middle of the dance floor (if you have one) on your wedding day and observe this once in a lifetime event happening all around you and be present through it all.

- You will tell the story of your wedding day through the elements that you make a priority.
- You will tell the story of your wedding day through the way your values align with your wedding planning decisions.

- You will tell the story of your wedding day
  through how you make your guests feel.

Ultimately the story is told by focusing on who you are and how you want to feel, then turning that into the wedding of your dreams, making it memorable and meaningful — like all the best stories are.

This isn't like every other wedding planning book.

I am as concerned as you about how to make your wedding different and how to make it meaningful. You are unique, and your wedding should be too. This means you won't find ideas about which seat cover to choose or how much beer you need. Your wedding is about you, and generic beer and wine quantity suggestions won't be relevant to *your* friends and *your* family. The same for seat covers. What you might need will depend on what chairs are at *your* venue. So generic advice will miss the mark and it won't feel relevant to *you*. Instead, this book will help you to clarify how you want your wedding to feel and what story you want to tell with your wedding. Then it will show you how to turn these into actions.

- This book will help you make your wedding
  unique by teaching you to focus on the details.
  The details will build the big picture.
- This book will help you make your wedding
  different by teaching you to look at your wedding
  from new perspectives. You can build a wedding
  based on your priorities rather than what the
  industry dictates you *should* have. You will start to
  see how 'personalised' and 'meaningful' are way
  better than 'traditional' and 'standard'.

Have you ever hosted a party and then realised you're not even enjoying it because you're trying to make sure everyone else is okay? It gets to the end of the night and you are secretly so happy the party is over so you can slip off your heels and disappear alone. *Please* don't let your wedding be like this. Be happy, be relaxed and carefree!

Plan for how you want to *feel* and notice the details.

That's the secret.

It doesn't matter if your wedding isn't for another ten years; these tools are timeless, and you can never be too prepared when it comes to wedding planning.

TWO

Why Are You Really Here?

You're here to plan your wedding, right? Which is great, but the thing that comes straight after a wedding is a marriage.

It's really important that you keep this in the forefront of your mind. It sounds so simple, but it's easy to forget that weddings and marriage come hand in hand.

You are planning the celebration that signifies the start of a marriage — a forever after. So, when you are losing your mind over your bridesmaids' inability to choose a dress, or your mother-in-law's unhelpful comments about cake flavours and edits (and more edits) to your seating plan — you can stop and remember you are planning for a marriage, *not just a wedding*.

As soon as that sparkling ring hits your left hand, you'll hear a chorus of: "When's the wedding?". Roll with the excitement but don't ever forget the real reason for the celebration.

The real reason you are talking about colour schemes and wedding themes is because you would like to spend the rest of your life with someone. That is huge. And it's important you spend some time reflecting on this. Often this gets lost, but really, it's the most important thing. This is why I wanted to start with this; let's keep it as your top priority.

Marriage first, then the wedding.

By focusing on why you are really planning a wedding you will:

- Plan the wedding you really want and not get swept away.
- Make your wedding more personal.
- Save money by cutting out some of the elements that are 'just for show'.
- Make your wedding different from everyone else's. It will be about you and your journey.
- Find it easier to make decisions as you'll have a clear focus.

Activity One

LOVE LETTERS

Take some time to write a love letter to your partner. Let them know what you are looking forward to the *most* about getting married.

Write to them about why you want this day to be so special and why you are putting so much energy into getting it 'just right'.

Tell them what you are looking forward to about spending the rest of your lives together. If you aren't getting married yet, that's okay — you don't have to send this letter, it can be kept just for you as a reminder for future years. It can help you focus on the real reasons for the wedding.

Buy a really lovely card from a really posh card shop, the sort you only go in occasionally, or start crafting and make a DIY card. Even if you just use multicoloured pens on a blank sheet of A4, take some time out of your busy week to let your future husband or wife know exactly how special they are and why you really want to plan a wedding — to get married.

If you are struggling to start, try these prompts.

Love letter prompts:

- The top ten reasons why I want to marry you...
- Our whole wedding day will be special, but I'm looking forward to this part the most...
- I want our wedding to reflect the things I love about our relationship. These are...
- If I could sum up what our future marriage means to me in one word, it would be...
- This is what marriage means to me...
- When I imagine marrying you, this is what it looks like...
- In ten years' time, I hope our life looks like this...
- You are special to me because...
- I want to put lots of energy into this part of our wedding...
- This is how much you mean to me...

Next, pop your card in the post and watch your partner's reaction when they open it. Above all else, this is what matters – your choice to spend the rest of your life with someone. When things get stressful, or if something doesn't work out as planned, remember this is the reason you started to plan a wedding, because you're planning for a marriage.

THREE

What is a DIY Wedding Anyway?

So, what does a DIY wedding mean anyway?

Do it yourself, *of course.*

The truth is all weddings are DIY. It's just the extent of the DIY that's up to you!

Even if some couples think they don't want a DIY wedding, most elements in a wedding still need some sort of 'bringing together'. Some parts can't be outsourced, and you don't have much choice other than to 'do it yourself'.

But a DIY wedding can have multiple meanings, and this is where things can get a little confusing. A DIY wedding can mean everything is handmade and crafted at home, this is perhaps a more traditional definition, that's had its fair share of criticism over the years. Or it can mean that you buy a wedding package from a hotel, but you still have to piece together the details and add all the elements that aren't included – the dress, the cars, the rings. It can mean you create a venue from scratch, literally putting up a marquee or tying together a church and a village hall. It can mean cooking all the food yourself and getting family to serve drinks. Or deciding which caterer you want and figuring out if they will work at your venue. There are many variations on the exact definition of a DIY wedding. There isn't one right answer.

But this is exciting. It means you get to choose how much DIY you want or don't want.

There is a lot to planning any wedding. It doesn't matter what extent of 'DIY-NESS' you choose to implement; it just matters that it is right for you and that you are organised.

To me, DIY means no rules. That is why I personally opted for a DIY wedding and why I encourage others to go for DIY venues, because no one will tell you what wine you can or can't drink. No one will tell you what time things have to start or end, and you can eat whatever food you want! There are no rules. But it's not for everyone, and that's okay too.

People choose a DIY wedding for many reasons:

- **To save money** – This is one of the biggest reasons people often choose DIY. We will talk about this in more length later because DIY can mean saving money, but DIY weddings can also be very expensive. Small things can add up and I've seen budgets run out of control. But if you're thrifty, focus on your priorities and are budget savvy, you can definitely save money by having a DIY wedding.
- **To create things** – People choose DIY because they can spend months and years making and crafting, sewing and building beautiful decorations

for their wedding. What better way to spend rainy evenings? You can put feelings and meaning into lovingly crafted wedding decorations and favours, and that is a great reason to choose a DIY wedding.

- **To keep busy** – Weddings can be stressful and can lead to anxiety. They are such a huge change in people's lives, so keeping busy in the lead-up to the big day can be a great tool to deal with the emotional experience. DIY weddings will keep you very busy!

- **More personal reasons** – Often people choose a DIY wedding because it might be a good opportunity to spend quality time with family or friends. It could allow family members to feel more involved and be a part of your wedding; it is such a unique opportunity to bring people together.

- **To have more control** – There is no doubt about it, DIY weddings are a lot of work, and this is because you are completely in control. You get to make all the decisions. This is such an incredible opportunity for you to bring your vision to life. You get to make huge decisions and build something that is just for you. It's wonderful getting to make all the decisions and seeing the results of your work will be very rewarding.

It's important to realise that every element of a wedding can be DIY if you let it and if you want it to be. *Everything* can be DIY. For example:

If you want to save money on photography, it can be a DIY element. You can provide guests with cameras and ask them to take pictures. Or you can buy mid-range professional camera and ask a trusted friend to take pictures, or you could just press record on a camera and let the day play out.

DIY is about breaking the rules. It literally means *doing it yourself*, your way. If you want to 'DIY' any element of your wedding, you can. Just because others don't doesn't matter. This freedom is why DIY weddings can be the most rewarding.

This also means you have decisions to make.

Activity Two

Why are <u>you</u> choosing to have a DIY wedding?

Grab a blank piece of paper and create three columns. Add one of the following statements to the top of each column.

- *I am planning a DIY wedding because...*
- *The things I really want to make/plan myself are...*
- *The people I have around me to help are...*

Start to answer the statements in each column with your partner.

What does DIY mean to you?

Spend some time talking about why you have chosen to go down the DIY route. Then think about the elements you really want to DIY. Is it the flowers? Or would you love to make your very own wedding cake? Or is it more about having a DIY venue that allows you to have more control?

You can't do everything; that's why it's good to ensure you are reflecting on the items that are the most important to you, the things you really want to make yourselves. You can then make space in your plans to ensure you don't run out of time to make the DIY elements of your wedding that you really care about.

Top Tip – It might also be worth asking family and friends for their input at this stage. Do you have a friend who wants to make your flowers? Or does a parent want to help with your wedding cake?

Take some time to really think about what DIY means to you.

FOUR

Feelings Matter

You are now focused on why you are planning a wedding
(for marriage) and you've decided DIY is for you, the next
logical place to move on to might be wedding timelines, or
budgets, or colour schemes, but we aren't tackling those
yet. We are going to continue with feelings. All the squishy,
emotional, hard to describe things. The feelings will make
your wedding unique.

I'll explain.

Have you this read this quote before?

> "*I've learned that people will forget what you said, people will
> forget what you did, but people will never forget how you made
> them feel.*"
>
> — Maya Angelou.

This quote is not only true for relationships, but it's also
true for weddings!

Your guests won't remember what your centrepieces looked like, or what colour your confetti was, even though it seems like an important decision now. But they will remember how they *felt* at your wedding reception, or how they *felt* when they saw you walk down the aisle. They will remember the fun they had and the stories that were created.

It's the same for you too.

Believe it or not, in ten years' time, you might not even remember the song you played for your first dance, the hymns you sang or the wine you served. But you will remember how you felt when you walked into the reception room for the first time, or how you felt when you saw your partner for the first time at the end of the aisle. You'll remember these feelings. So, this is what we'll explore next, by talking about how you want your wedding to *feel*.

Why do feelings matter?

This is important for a few reasons:

- **Because feelings will stick in your memories.** There is a lot of research that shows we remember events, moments and memories for longer when emotions are attached to them. This is because of our emotional memory[1]. You'll want to remember your wedding day forever, so if you can cement feelings into the different parts of your day, not only will it be more meaningful but you'll remember the details for longer.
- **Feelings lead to decisions**. You are going to have to make lots of decisions over the next few

weeks and months as you plan your wedding. And if you know how you want to *feel* on your wedding day, it can lead to clearer decision making, specifically when you know how you want to feel at different moments of your wedding. It can mean the difference between making decisions because you feel pressured or forced, or listening to your heart and going with your gut, knowing you've already committed to a set path. With the amount of decisions you're going to need to make over the next few months, you'll want them all to be as easy as possible.

- **If you are clear on how you want to feel on your wedding day, it's much easier to plan everything else**. Once you have feelings nailed other wedding elements seem to matter less; you plan based on emotions and create meaningful wedding moments rather than creating expensive photo opportunities.

- **If things go wrong, you will know which feelings matter more.** For example, if your flowers are the wrong colour on the wedding day or one of the members of the band is sick, and they send a replacement, you won't care because you will still feel calm and your guests will still feel loved and cared for. You will know it's *those* feelings that matter more than the colour of your flowers. It allows you to prioritise and reduce stress.

Let me explain.

Feelings run deeper than appearances.

Have you ever been to a wedding that you know cost thousands of pounds? It was most likely in the perfect location, the sun shone, the drinks flowed. Yet it felt staged somehow? Dare we say *boring*? Perhaps the time dragged? Or was it predictable? Were you counting down the hours until you could go home?

This could be a case of that wedding focusing on *looks* rather than feeling.

You can create a perfect-looking wedding, but if you've forgotten to factor in how you want to feel, how you want your guests to feel, it will be missing something key. The perfect venue and the expensive dress won't cover up for a lack of emotion and personalisation. Venues come and go, but weddings that reflect the essence of who a couple are and what they love, those weddings don't drag.

Those weddings are remembered forever.

Questions to consider:

- Have you been to a wedding before? How many can you remember off the top of your head? What were they like?
- Can you think about some of the elements of those weddings that you remember the most? What sticks out?
- What parts of the wedding day did you enjoy?
- How did the wedding make you feel? Was there an overarching emotion that stuck? Did it feel really personal? Did it feel like an incredible party? Did you feel awkward because it was very formal? Or was it disorganised? What was the one feeling that summed it up?
- Now, can you think of a favourite wedding you've been to? Why this wedding? What made it stand out?

- What feelings would you like to emulate from other weddings you've attended in your own wedding?

When we talk about feelings, we are talking about the emotions you want to experience on your wedding day. Yes, you will want to feel happy, but think deeper than that. Be more specific.

Here is an example:

> *"I want to feel surrounded by people who love me. I want to allow people to feel part of the day. I want to feel calm. I want to feel… thankful, joyful, grateful and peaceful."*

Be really specific. Pick values and words that mean something to you. If you can articulate exactly how you want to feel, you have a much greater chance of attaining these feelings. Your brain likes to close loops; if you start to feed images and description into your brain, it will work with you to try and make these things happen. To close the loops.

Other examples could include:

> *"I want my guests to feel spoiled and looked after. I want to shower them with hospitality."*

> *"I want to feel like a king/queen for the day. I want the attention to be on me and I want to feel special."*

> *"I want to feel completely myself and comfortable in how I look. I want to feel proud of what I've built with my partner."*

"I want to feel in control. I want my guests to feel like everything is well planned and organised so they can relax."

"I want to feel excited. I want to feel loved and I want my guests to feel loved too. I want to feel like I've smiled all day."

There is no right or wrong answer, it's just important you are really honest with yourself and your partner. It's your day. Make sure you feel how you want to feel.

Important note: Just because you may not have 'felt' a certain way at a wedding you've attended, it doesn't mean the bride and groom didn't have the wedding of their dreams. Weddings are personal; there shouldn't be judgement, just learning from experiences, borrowing ideas and weaving inspiration into your wedding plans from any source. We are not here to criticise other weddings, just learn from them.

Activity Three

WHAT FEELINGS DO YOU WANT?

Set a timer for five minutes and write down some of the key 'feelings' you would like to have in all the different parts of your wedding day. It's important to do this with a timer at first, as it forces you to be quick, and this means you are working with your gut reaction. You can always go back and spend some more time fleshing out the specifics, but often your gut reaction and first choice speaks the most truth.

Feelings questions:

- What is the overarching feeling you would like to have on your wedding day?
- Could you summarise your whole wedding day feelings with three emotions/feelings?
- At key moments during your wedding day how do you want to feel? Summarise them with a few emotions and words.
- How do you want to feel when you are walking

down the aisle? During the wedding breakfast? At the reception?

- How do you want your guests to feel?
- And what about after your wedding? Think about how you want to feel. Do you want to feel relaxed or exhausted from dancing all night? How do you want to feel when you wake up on the morning after your wedding?

Don't forget to talk to your partner too and get their opinion. How do they want to feel? Do they agree with what you've written, or is it quite different? Do your feelings match up? Think about how you want them to feel too, how do you want them to experience the wedding day? What do you want for them?

It's important you can both openly talk about how you want to feel and you work towards similar if not matching feelings.

FIVE

Goals. Goals. Goals.

Feelings are great. But you need to put actions behind them to make them a reality.

You need to start laying the foundations for your wedding planning. You need goals. If you can articulate your feelings into goals, you can then work towards achieving them. These goals will then inform all of your wedding decision making.

These first goals should directly relate to the feelings you want to experience. Setting goals will help with your wedding planning because:

- They will clarify your feelings.
- They will create focus.
- They will allow you to visualise what you really want.

These goals need to be specific. With this type of goal setting, you are also manifesting how you want to feel.

Manifesting is simply putting enough thought into something so you can clearly describe it. Then you can clearly explain what you want. Manifesting wedding goals in this way allows you to focus on what you really want, and then you are one step closer to turning it into a reality.

Gabby Bernstein describes manifesting on her popular blog gabbyberstien.com:

> *"Manifesting is cultivating the experience of what it is that you want to feel — then living and believing in that experience so that you can allow it to come into form."*[1]

We are aiming for you to be able to visualise the exact wedding you want to build by creating goals around how you want to feel. It sounds complicated, but really it's just describing exactly how you want to feel and matching it with actions. This builds upon your ability to clarify the wedding you *really* want rather than build a wedding that looks great.

The next activity will help you set these goals.

Activity Four

Grab a large blank piece of paper, or open up a new blank text document on your computer.

Write down your overarching wedding day feeling that you've uncovered from activity three, and some of the other feelings you want to experience, at the top of the page. Then draw three columns.

Add the following titles to the columns:

- On my wedding day I will feel…
- On our wedding day we both want to feel…
- I want my guests and family to feel…

Set a goal under each heading that relates to the feelings you want to create and experience.

For example:

1. On my wedding day I will feel…

Feeling: Relaxed.

Goal: "I will feel well and full of energy on my wedding day. I will feel calm and relaxed, I won't lift a finger because everything will be well planned and delegated."

2. On our wedding day we both want to feel…

Feeling: Protected.

Goal: "On our wedding day we will both feel special but not the centre of attention. We will feel like our guests are having a great time and we will feel that our wedding reflects our values. We won't do anything we don't want to do."

3. I want my guests and family to feel…

Feeling: Supported.

Goal: "Our guests will feel loved. Our family will feel like they have a part to play in our wedding, as they play a huge part in our lives. Our guests will feel like they are actively involved in our wedding and they will feel like we appreciate them. We will show this through serving excellent food and drinks."

This task will help you to refine your goals and make them clearer as you go through the planning stages. It also helps to start to make your feelings actionable. It may take some time to turn your ideas into practical actions, but that's okay. This is about refining your ideas and getting clear on your goals.

SIX

Priorities v Expectations

Now you've thought about how you want to feel it leads us onto your priorities. What matters *most* to you? You can start to see how the goal setting is helping to highlight your priorities and how these can be turned into focused actions.

Notice we are looking at feelings, goals and priorities before we get to the '*rustic, boho, festival, fairy-tale*' wedding buzzwords that you'll find surrounding wedding planning. Themes are great. And if one of those words is your 'feeling', and you can describe it as part of your wedding goals, then that's fine. But just as 'buzzwords', they don't mean anything.

For example, you could have a beautiful rustic wedding cake, but if you've already decided you don't really care about the wedding cake and it's not one of your priorities, it doesn't matter that you can get one for £900 and it fits with your theme. You could have spent that money on something that really fitted how you wanted to *feel* rather than a wedding extra that looks good. Don't get me wrong, cake is great, but a cake for £30 from a local bakery is just as delicious.

You might want your wedding to *feel* like a festival because your goal is:

"To reunite our family, having all my friends and family camp in our own little festival village, so we can maximise our time together, as we don't get together often."

The difference is you are deciding to create a feeling and a goal rather than a *look* or a *theme.* For the example above, it's really about stretching out the event to spend more time with loved ones — that's the real priority.

Your priorities

Feelings can help you create your wedding priorities.

As soon as you get engaged, people will be excited. Family will want to chip in with ideas, thoughts and, worse, expectations.

- Just because your sister got married at the local church doesn't mean you have to.
- Just because your mum wants you to wear her grandmother's veil doesn't mean you should.
- Just because everyone has a wedding breakfast doesn't mean you have to.

What you want matters. What is important is working with your partner to be really clear on this, so you can show and tell other people. Bring them on this journey with you.

Ignore expectations for now; these will cloud your vision, and this will force you into a prescribed wedding. I want to talk about *your* priorities. You might find these are obvious to you, or you might have started to uncover some surprises.

What do you care about most when you think of your wedding?

You know you haven't got an unlimited budget, so what do you really *really* want? Try not to think about what you should or shouldn't do, just about what really matters to you.

The wedding world will tell you there are many items that are absolutely necessary for you to have at a wedding:

- Videographer
- Photographer
- Photobooth
- Donut wall (?!)
- Large bridal party
- Expensive, unique favours
- An open bar
- Wedding planner
- Two wedding dresses/two suits.

Tradition will also demand you must have certain elements for a wedding to even count:

- A fancy car
- A big church wedding
- A wedding breakfast
- Lots of long speeches
- A first dance

- A bouquet toss
- A string quartet.

And expectations from family or Pinterest might even tell you that certain elements are needed for your wedding to be classed as 'good':

- Welcome cocktails
- Garden games
- A live band
- Big blowout stag and hen party celebrations
- Sparklers.

This is a <u>big</u> lie.

None of these elements have to be a part of your wedding. They don't have to be your priority.

All you really need is a partner who wants to get married and a legal ceremony. Believe it or not, you don't need anything else.

Strip back your dusty old-fashioned wedding beliefs and give yourself time to think, with no pressure about what *you* actually want. Think about what *you* care about. It's fine if you want all of those items listed above, just make sure it's what you want and not what the world demands you should have.

The aim is to prioritise the wedding elements you want to focus on.

You can't prioritise it all. Your priorities list will help you understand where you might have to make compromises too, should budget or other circumstances demand this. It's great to reflect back on this list of priorities when you come to look at budgeting. If you want the expensive shoes, you might have to compromise on the cake or the canapés, for example.

It doesn't matter what your priorities are as long as *you know* what matters to you. You will need to use these priorities throughout the rest of the book, so it's important you spend some time getting clear on what they are.

Activity Five

TELL ME WHAT YOU WANT, WHAT YOU REALLY REALLY WANT?

This next activity explains how you can discover your priorities. Looking at:

- Necessity v Luxury.
- Traditions v The 'Real You'.
- Expectations v Priorities.

In ten years' time, what will you remember from your wedding day? What do you *want* to remember?

Below are lots of elements and feelings that can (but don't have to) make up a wedding:

- Music
- Food
- Joy
- The dress
- Photography
- Entertainment
- Accommodation

- A weekend-long celebration
- The guest list
- Creativity
- Canapés
- Invitations
- Shoes
- Open bar
- Romance
- Traditional
- Laughter
- Family-focused
- Hen/stag party
- Low-key
- Flowers
- The suits
- Videography
- Emotional
- Inspiring
- Hair and make-up
- Friends
- Elegant
- Relaxed
- The cake
- Wild party
- DIY decorations
- Simple
- Peaceful
- The rings
- Detail-orientated
- Formal
- The wedding cars
- Church
- Afterparty
- Band

- DJ
- Amazing food
- Fun
- Honeymoon
- Thoughtful
- Amazing venue.

Your task:

1. Circle ten of the items on the list that really matter to you. If you can, make sure they link in with your feelings and wedding goals. If you think there are some items missing, feel free to add your own elements. This is in no way a prescriptive list, nor is it exhaustive; it's a start to help you identify your priorities.

2. Sit with your partner and get them to do the same. Do any of your priorities overlap? Are you both set on a weekend-long celebration with an open bar? Or are your priorities way off? Is one of you wanting an intimate ceremony abroad? Focus in on the feelings.

3. Go back through your list and narrow it down to your top eight priorities, things that you really care about and want to include in your wedding. Circle these with a different coloured pen.

4. Now go back again and narrow it down to your top five priorities. Use a different coloured pen again. It should feel like a difficult task, because you care about all of these elements, but it's about nailing down the most important elements so they can become your priority.

5. Next, go back to the original list. Cross out five to ten elements that aren't your priorities, the things

you really aren't too bothered about. This doesn't mean you are scrapping them from your wedding completely, it just means you might be happy to use your friend's car for a lift to the ceremony rather than paying £550 for a five-minute ride in a limo or a Bentley just because your dad used to like that sort of car. This is about prioritising what *you* care about, not what others *expect* you to have. Let these items become zero budget items or move them to the bottom of the to-do list. Ask yourself if you really need them as part of your wedding day?

P.S If you want a five-minute ride in a Bentley because your dad used to be a professional driver and you know riding with him in the car would be such a special memory, then do it and ride around the wedding venue twice.

P.P.S If you want Christian Louboutin shoes for your wedding day because you would never dream of spending that sort of money at any other time, that's okay. You should have what you want. Those shoes can be a priority, if that's what you want. It doesn't matter what your priorities are, as long as you know they are what matter to *you*.

It's okay to plan the exact wedding you want.

By the end of this task you should now have a list of your top five priorities, and a list of five elements that are not a priority.

SEVEN

The Magic Formula

We've looked at the most important reason for your wedding, the feelings you want to experience and now you have identified your priorities and what you want to focus on.

When you add these elements together, you are able to create your wedding vision statement, and *this is gold!* A wedding vision statement is a succinct definition of your wedding. This is where the magic happens.

The Magic Formula

The Marriage!
(Your reason for wedding planning in the first place.)

+

Your Feelings
(A clear understanding of how you want to feel on your wedding day and what this might look like as actionable goals.)

+

A Priorities List
(The things you really care about.)

= Your wedding vision statement

Here's a wedding vision statement example:

> *"Our wedding will be a loud crazy party with all our friends and family. We will feel relaxed and carefree. We love music and want our wedding to reflect the way we feel about this, with our priorities being live bands and a venue with a big dance floor. We want to dance our way into our marriage."*

You can almost feel that wedding, can't you? You start to build a picture in your mind of exactly what that day might be like. If you shared that statement with someone else, they could have a good understanding of what matters to that couple too.

That's the sort of statement you need. Think of your vision statement as a way of describing your wedding's personality.

It is so important you are able to clarify your wedding vision statement for lots of reasons. Not only does it summarise the hard work you've put in with your partner to nail down the 'why' and the 'what', but it can also be really useful when dealing with suppliers, family or the expectations of others. It is a statement of intent. The ultimate goal and a workable target. You need to share this with everyone. Stick it on your notice board, send it with your invites, email it to your suppliers and be really clear when making any decisions about your wedding that it needs to fit with your statement.

You can get really creative with how you share it with others. You'll find it trickling into all of your plans, decorations and even your theme. It will seep into every element of your wedding, and that's exactly how it should be.

Let me explain further why you need a wedding vision statement and why everyone needs to see it.

- **Suppliers**. This could be your photographer, wedding planner, caterer or even your venue. They all need to grasp what matters to *you*, what is important and meaningful to *you*. They need to have a clear understanding of your wedding vision statement, because they should be working towards it too! Be clear with them so they understand *your* dream. Sell them *your* vision so they don't make assumptions, so they don't try and squeeze *your* wedding into the box of other people's weddings. We are here to create weddings that break the mould. You are unique. Your wedding should be too.

- **Family**. Your family need to know your wedding vision statement so they can understand your decision-making process. They need to know your *why* and they need to be on board with your decisions so they can make your wedding about you. About *your* feelings and *your* relationship. So, when your Aunty Jane takes you to a country manor house you can tell her *"no, there is no space for a tipi here. It won't work because I want to feel free on my wedding day and to do that I need to be outside."* (Hint: This is where you show her your vision statement.) Your vision statement will give you the confidence you need to shout from the rooftops about what you want, because it's based on your feelings, your heart, and that's what matters. Your family will see that, and they will love it because they will realise the essence of your wedding and the decisions you make are based on who you are and your efforts to create a meaningful wedding.

- **Budget**. When you are in a Pinterest spiral and you think you might need personalised wedding CDs for all your guests to take home, stop and take a look at your vision statement. You can take a step back and see that you don't need personalised CDs. In fact, you don't even need favours if you don't want them. Remind yourself you wanted your wedding to feel like a party, and to do that you need more money for your bar, so you've scrapped favours and moved the money to drinks. When in doubt, before pressing pay, refer to your vision statement.

- **When you get lost in the whirlwind**. Your wedding vision statement allows you to come back to the heart of your wedding. The reasons why you started. So, when you are knee-deep in making invites or worrying about seating plans, you can remember the elements that matter.

You will soon know your wedding vision statement is ultimately the thing you want your guests to say about your wedding, their lasting memory — you just hadn't even realised it.

Activity Six

YOUR WEDDING VISION STATEMENT

Use the magic formula to make your wedding vision statement.

Go and sit somewhere with your partner — take yourselves out to a nice coffee shop or bar. Or just turn off Netflix for one night and sit at the kitchen table with a bottle of wine and create your wedding vision statement together.

Add up the reasons why you want to get married, with the overarching feelings and goals you've set. Then add in the wedding elements that are your priorities and you've got yourself a wedding statement.

Play around with some of the sentences from your feeling goals, link in your priorities, think about your relationship and the things you love. Write a vision statement for your wedding based on these priorities.

You can write your final version on a small card. Or you can get creative and design a fun version on your computer or use some good old-fashioned magazine cut-outs and Sharpies. Keep the statement close, stick it to your wedding planning notebook or keep in your purse, but refer back to it when you are making wedding decisions.

The vision statement can be really detailed, or it can be more open-ended if you are still making decisions, but it's important it reflects you and how you want your wedding to be. Think about the story you want to tell with your wedding. How do you want it to be remembered? Try and add this to your vision statement too.

Here's a few examples to help you get started:

Our Wedding Vision Statement: *"An example of love in action. Our wedding will feel like a huge gathering of our most favourite people in the world — happiness, stories and peaceful joy. We will feel full of gratitude and thankfulness. We will make the people we love feel special and a huge part of our day. This day will set the standard for the rest of our lives. Palms open, big love, big laughs, big stories and memory making fun."*

Our Wedding Vision Statement: *"Our wedding will reflect the love we feel towards each other with a religious ceremony that represents our faith. We want it to feel intimate and small, with just our close family. We want our wedding to feel small, private and formal to reflect the seriousness of our decision to spend our lives together."*

Our Wedding Vision Statement: *"After finding each other through a second chance at love, we want our wedding to feel like a gift. We want to make our friends and family feel looked after and special. We want to feel relaxed and to this end we will have a wedding that is catered with the highest standards of food and drink. These elements will be our priority, with drinks served at the table."*

Part One Summary

You've worked hard to hash out the real feelings you want to experience on your wedding day, and hopefully you've now got a wedding statement that reflects the real 'you'.

Everyone likes the sound of a rustic English garden wedding with shabby chic decorations and afternoon tea. But do you know what they like even more? A wedding that epitomises the love the couple feel for each other, shown through a wedding day that truly reflects the couple as they are and what they love. A real love story.

To summarise this section:

- You have reflected on your 'real reasons' for getting married or planning a special day.
- You have a crystal-clear idea about what a DIY wedding means to you.
- You have worked to ensure you have a clear plan for how you would like your wedding day to feel.
- You have looked at how having clear goals for your big day will allow you to defy expectations

(and Pinterest) and build a wedding that reflects who you really are.

- You have built a wedding vision statement based on your feelings, values and priorities.

Now you've completed the groundwork, and the vision is clear, in the next part we can talk about venues, suppliers and catering, as you'll know if this fits with your feelings and priorities.

Activity Seven

You've made it to the end of the first part of this book and it's time for some homework. I'd advise completing this before you move to the next section. These tasks will keep you focused and allow you to process all of the information that's been covered, and it will help you to contextualise it. It's also going to be fun.

Capture the feelings, vision statement and priorities you've decided on by designing a wedding mood board!

You can make your mood board on Pinterest, or it can be a paper and glue cut-out, even a PowerPoint! Whatever speaks to you! Have fun, go crazy and throw on some glitter. Ensure your mood board reflects your feelings, vision statement and priorities!

Ensure you speak with your partner and make sure they are happy and fully in agreement with the vision statement and priorities. Show them the mood board too, or even make it together. Having a clear visual for your wedding day helps make it even clearer in your head too.

Don't forget to show your mood board to your suppliers!

Top Tip - Why not get your bridesmaids or family to make a mood board with you, especially if they aren't quite on board with your vision? It could be a good way to talk about your ideas.

Part Two – Exploring Your Options

EIGHT

The Four Lies of Wedding Planning

"What do you mean you are getting married *this* summer? Don't you need at least two years to plan a *proper* wedding?"

I've overhead many conversations similar to this. Wedding fairs are ripe with excited and helpful friends who want to pour out all the advice they've heard, or read on Pinterest.

"We got married and only spent £200 pounds!"

Glossy pins, magazine articles, blogs and Facebook ads might lure you in with catchy headlines and clickbait.

"Well when I got married, we did it this way and you MUST do this too…"

Helpful ex-brides sharing unsolicited advice. Well-meaning but misplaced, perhaps?

When you know what you want, it doesn't matter what the world states you should have. It's easy to get pulled into conversations and opinions, though.

Talking about DIY weddings brings up lots of questions. But it also brings up lots of lies. I want to talk to you about the four lies of wedding planning. You will see and hear these all of the time, and it's really easy to get sucked into believing them and even hearing yourself say them. The wedding industry is built on money, rules and traditions. But we know it should be built on feelings, stories and priorities. These are the most common lies I've heard, and we are going to debunk some of the myths and discover the truths.

LIE #1 – You can't have a wedding for over 100 people on a budget.

The Truth: You can have 250 people at your wedding and the real truth is you *can* do it on a budget. The difference is you might not be eating a three-course roast dinner, but if it means the world to you to have everyone you know there, you can do it. I promise. Don't listen to the lie of the wedding guest myth. You can have as many people as you want, you just need to look at what needs to give to make this happen.

The number of guests you invite can be a sticking point for people; it can stop you from inviting some of your very best friends because the food you've chosen costs too much. But it's all just about priorities. Nobody minds eating pizza for lunch.

Do you want the venue or the people? The people or the nice food?

It's not really about compromising; it's about understanding your priorities. The people who love you will show up, even if it's just for the evening and even if there is no food. Don't feel like you have to believe the lie that you can't invite who you want to your wedding. There will always be a way. Don't feel like you have to cut your guest list to save money. You can cut back on other elements if the guest list is your priority. You just have to be clear on your priorities. Know what you want.

LIE #2 - DIY means my wedding will be cheaper.

I'm sorry, but this is a huge lie. Maybe even the biggest lie.

Sometimes DIY can be cheaper, yes. You can definitely have a DIY wedding on a budget, and it will be beautiful. But not always.

Most of the time, it's definitely *not* cheaper. But that's okay, because that is not always why people chose a DIY wedding.

The DIY difference is that it gives you more flexibility to make some elements cheaper, if that's what you want. But it also allows you to have *all* of the elements that you want. It allows you to be in control. It gives you so much more choice. It gives you flexibility. Flexibility lets you align priorities. For example, you could choose a DIY venue and it could be more expensive than a hotel venue. But the payoff might mean that everyone can stay over in glamping tents and that is cheaper than putting everyone up in a hotel. Or you can save money and food and wine as you can provide it all yourself. But if one of your priorities was to have all your guests staying over, then it's a win-win. With the glamping, everyone stays over and gets 'free' accommodation. So you could ask them all to bring a buffet lunch item and seventy-six guest buffet lunch items equals a wedding breakfast.

It's all about the payoff and the priority. What matters more to you? These are tough questions but spending the time to get to the heart of your wedding will be worth it.

LIE #3 - You must have certain elements to call a wedding a 'wedding'.

"You're not having a cake?"
"What do you mean, no bridesmaids?"
"But you *have* to have a DJ!'

No. These are all lies too.

The truth is, if you don't want a wedding cake, you don't have to have one. If you don't want a wedding car, use a taxi. If you don't want bridesmaids, you don't need them. We've talked about the elements that make up a wedding, they are very simple: two people who want to spend the rest of their lives together, a ceremony of commitment and *that's it*. Everything else is extra. Even the people are extra, especially if they are going to stress you out.

You get to break all the rules with a DIY wedding, and that's why you'll love it.

If you don't want favours or balloons or speeches, you don't need them. You don't have to have them. If you don't want the tradition of a first dances and a garter toss, or a receiving line, you don't have to have them.

It's your wedding and you can design it exactly how you want it to be. Take this to heart.

LIE #4 - You can have it all.

The truth about your wedding is that you can't have it all, which I realise might be an unpopular opinion.

But it's okay, because the real truth is, you don't need it all. Your marriage is the all. That will be the make or break, that will be the everything, the all. Your wedding is just the epic start of that.

I mean you can have it all if you're mega-rich and budget or time aren't issues. But if not, you can't have it all. Yet if you know what your priorities are it doesn't matter, because it will *feel* like you've got it all.

For example:

If you don't care about your cake, it won't make you happier to buy one that fits with your theme for £1,730. You'll will just think "*oh that looks nice*" for about five minutes. But if you really care about your cake and you forego the favours to pay for it, oh my goodness you are going to admire that cake. You are going to wish you didn't have to cut into it. And it will feel perfect, because it will feel like you've got what you *really* want. Plus, you can always cut the cake up, pop the pieces in a nice box and hey — you've got favours!

Do you see the difference?

So what does it mean, having it all?

Every idea and picture you've seen on Pinterest, every element from a friend's wedding that you want to steal, every tradition, every idea — that's what we mean by having it all. The extras.

But the things that will *really* make you happy, and the things that will turn *your* wedding into a story, are the priorities you've *already* highlighted. These are the parts that really matter to you. And when you've got those elements, it will feel like you've got it all.

Focus on planning your priorities and you'll have the day of your dreams.

NINE

The Chicken or the Egg?

Even with clear priorities it can be very difficult to know where to start with wedding planning because there is so much to do, but also because one thing leads to another. It's a process.

In the process you can't always move forward until you have confirmed the first steps. Yet identifying this process is very personal and depends on your priorities. That's why we started this book with them, but where do you go next?

Believe it or not, we've already covered a lot a ground. We've already started by working out your wedding foundations. Even though it might not feel like it, you have already gone a long way to planning the wedding of your dreams and making it different from everybody else's.

This is where the chicken and the egg comes into it. Do you decide on your venue first or your budget? The guest list or the food?

The planning process

I could list a carbon copy process that you should follow, but it wouldn't make your wedding different because it wouldn't be focused on what you really want. So, you need to design a bespoke process for you.

That's how you will determine where to go to next.

For example:

You could need to confirm:

- A wedding date
- Your budget
- The venue or location.

ALL FIRST.

This is where the chicken and the egg comes into it. It doesn't really matter.

All of those would be a great place to start, but the most important place to start is with what *matters to you*. This is why we have started to spend time on clarifying your priorities and feelings because that will equal your starting point.

I'll explain.

The things that make your wedding stand out won't be that you booked your photographer exactly one year to the day before your wedding, or that you sent out your wedding invites exactly nine months to the day before your wedding. It will be in the details and the unique differences, the things that make your wedding personal — and that is what I want to teach you through this book.

There are however, a few 'big things' that will help focus your wedding planning and create building blocks to move forward from. These are what I call the 'four pillars of wedding planning'.

The Four Pillars Of Wedding Planning

Pillar 1 – The Number of Wedding Guests
Pillar 2 – Your Budget
Pillar 3 – The Wedding Location or Venue
Pillar 4 – Your Wedding Date

Why are they called the four pillars?

Simply because every wedding has to have each one of these pillars and because they will determine your planning start line.

These pillars are the beginning of your wedding map. Your wedding planning process will be driven forward by one of these pillars in particular. You just need to figure out which one. Your wedding will include them all, but one will be a driver.

Let's break these pillars down some more so you start to see which pillar is your driver.

Wedding Location or Venue Pillar – If you really care about your venue you can start here, and you can book your wedding date based solely on when the venue is free. This is for people who are set on a particular venue, they know that's the place for them, and everything else has to work around the location.

The Number of Guests Pillar – Or if you want 250 people at your wedding you can start with your guest list and that can be your priority. You can then find a location that will hold everyone, and they can all bring a picnic. Just think, who do you love? Who must be there? Who do you still want in your life in ten years, twenty years? Who will support your marriage? And invite them all! The guest number will drive your decisions.

The Wedding Date Pillar – Are you set on a Saturday in August? Or a May bank holiday? Then perhaps your wedding date is unmovable and you need to work everything around this date. It becomes your priority. And you can focus on finding suppliers and a venue that are free on this date.

The Budget Pillar – Perhaps the budget is your priority and it is the element of planning you need to prioritise. If you've got a set figure in mind, then your wedding needs to work around this, not the other way around.

Knowing where to start with wedding planning can be really hard, but if you know which one of the wedding pillars in particular matters to you more, you can use that as your starting point. The next activity will help you establish further which wedding pillar might be your driver.

Don't forget to refer back to your goals, vision statement and priorities, you might have already decided on which pillar matters most to you. It might already be really obvious. This doesn't need to be a complicated process but it helps identify our next steps in your wedding planning and helps to give you a starting point.

Activity Eight

WHERE ARE YOU STARTING?

For this task you will be determining the wedding pillar that's leading your decision making.

Work through the questions, and be sure to go with your gut instinct — your first answers. Force yourself to choose from the either-or option.

Start a tally and list the number of times you chose a specific pillar as your answer. The pillar you pick the most frequently will be your priority and starting point.

These questions are designed to test your priorities and question what matters most to you. Some might seem repetitive because they really challenge your choices.

After that process you'll have the wedding pillar that is your priority. You can then fit all of the other wedding tasks and jobs around it, and this will be your starting point.

The chicken and egg theory with weddings is the idea that all elements are linked. They all need to be planned around each other. However, we are just trying to dig deeper into your priorities and looking to assess if one element of the wedding is more important to you, for example if you are planning to get married on a specific date. Don't worry if you can't decide between two pillars; they are all so closely linked sometimes there isn't one leading pillar.

If you don't keep your focus on these priorities it will be easy to get sucked into the pull and push of the wedding industry. It will be easy to fall for the scarcity idea, the idea and way of thinking that says there isn't enough to go around.

It's simply not true. *Scarcity isn't true*

Venues can get booked up two years in advance, but if you feel pressured into booking because you went on a venue show-around and they mentioned there are only a few dates left for next year, you might miss out on other venues that can host all of your guests. Focusing on what really matters will help you make clearer wedding decisions.

Uncovering your wedding pillar questions:

- Would you rather have all the guests you want or the venue of your dreams?

(Venue v Guest List)

- Do you still want the venue of your dreams if it means getting married on a weekday? *no.*

(Venue v Budget)

- Would you mind going over budget or delaying your wedding date to save more money, if it meant you got the venue you wanted?

(Venue v Budget)

- I don't mind foregoing the evening meal if it means we can have the venue we want.

(Venue v Budget) *meal*

- I want to get married abroad even if I know it means people won't be able to make it.

(Venue v Guest List) *not abroad*

- We can save X amount per month; this means our total budget will be Y. We can't stretch any more and budgeting is essential.

(Budget Pillar True/False)

- I don't want lots of people around me, I just want the perfect venue.

(Venue v Guest List)

- It's very important that all my friends attend, whatever the cost.

(Budget v Guest List)

- The venue is the most important thing, even if it means we compromise on dates or get married on a Monday.

(Venue v Date)

- I want the wedding to cost as little as possible.

(Budget Pillar True/False)

- Our wedding date is set because I want to get married in the summer.

(Date Pillar True/False)

- I don't mind getting married in five years if it means we can save more money and have the venue of our dreams.

(Venue v Date)

- I don't mind not inviting all my family if it means we stick to our budget.

(Budget v Guest List)

- The location of our venue is the most important thing.

(Venue v Guest List)

- I'm not worried about the venue if all my friends and family can come.

(Venue v Guest List)

- The date doesn't bother me as long as my friends can come.

(Date v Guest List)

- I have to get married on a Saturday.

(Date Pillar True/False)

Questions:

- Is there one pillar that sticks out?
- Does that feel like the right pillar for you?
- Are you set on a Saturday in June?
- Are you set on 119 people?
- Or is it more about your dream venue? The one you drive past every weekend?
- Or does none of this really matter because you've got a £5,000 budget and when it's gone, it's gone?

Don't forget all these elements do need to be planned, we're just trying to narrow down your priorities and really test if there is something that matters more to you, so you can plan that first.

Total up the number of times you have answered yes or chosen a specific wedding pillar. Let this be the place your start with your wedding planning. It's also okay if you find

Venue + Date + close friends.

everything is equally important, it just means you'll have to do more research in the next few stages.

TEN

What Next?

Having a clear idea of which wedding pillar matters the most to you means you can start to list the tasks you need to complete based on your main priority.

But first the big question:

How long does it really take to plan a wedding?

The short answer: as much or as little time as you've got.

Have you heard of Parkinson's Law? Parkinson's Law is usually expressed as:

"Work expands so as to fill the time available for its completion".

In other words, work grows and melts into all of the available time it's got. Cyril Parkinson first talked about this in an essay he wrote for *The Economist* in 1955[1]. Little did Cyril know his law has a lot to do with weddings.

If you have two years to plan a wedding, it will take you two years. If you have two months to plan, guess what? It will take you two months. Planning your wedding should be fun. It should give you a chance to be creative, and it should be an opportunity for you to enjoy designing your once in a lifetime event. For some people wedding planning can be stressful. Not giving yourself enough time to plan is one reason for this stress, or having too much time and adding lots of extras can also be a reason for the stress to pile up.

It's all about choices and priorities.

The more complicated your wedding, the more time you'll need. If you want to get married in two months, you can. Absolutely. But you might not have the time to delicately craft and create your own invites. You might not be able to make all the decorations yourself. However, if you do want to hand-stitch 100 fabric hearts for your favours, you're going to need a little bit of time, and you'll need to plan for that.

What are you happy to compromise on? Go back to your DIY list. What are you 100% set on having and how much time will that non-negotiable task take? Factor this into your planning timescale.

So how long do you really need?

According to *The Independent*, the average wedding takes 528 hours to plan[2], which is equivalent to fourteen weeks of full-time work. Crazy. But unbelievably fun. The last thing you want is to feel like you're running out of time. You don't want to be working around the clock in the last few weeks before your wedding.

The next stage of your wedding planning journey is the wedding planning timeline.

I've based the timeline template in this book on twelve months of wedding planning. Personally, I think that is the perfect amount of time to plan a wedding. I think twelve months gives you plenty of time, but you don't reach burn out, you don't get bored of your own ideas or lost along the way. You are focused and driven. However, I've known people to plan a whole wedding in six months or take three years, but for most people twelve months is plenty of time.

Of course, there are exceptions (venue, budget and suppliers). Don't be forced by any timeline you see. There are always workarounds, and it also depends on your budget and how quickly you can save.

For example:

You might have a supplier you need to book much further in advance – like the band that you LOVE. Or the venue you've got your heart set on, because you know it gets booked up two years in advance. Or if you need more time to reach your budget goals. It could be that twelve months isn't enough time to save up for your wedding.

If you know that these elements make up a priority for you, then of course you'll need to plan around this and factor in the lead time.

Let's dig further into your personal planning timeline.

Activity Nine

YOUR WEDDING TIMELINE

In this activity you will map out your wedding planning timeline.

You will find a list of all the 'standard' wedding jobs that need to be planned. I say 'standard' very cautiously, because I want to remind you it is not necessary to do all of these things. Just because they are on a standard list doesn't mean you have to include them. Go wild. Add your own ideas too. Take away elements. If the thought of homemade invites, PVA glue and glitter brings you stress, create a Facebook group to invite guests to your wedding or send a text invite.

Remember, there are no rules.

On a large piece of paper, or on a spreadsheet, start creating your own wedding planning timeline. Using this list as guide, move tasks around and add to it. List them in what you think is the right order based on *your* priorities.

Add the parts you think are missing and throw away the elements you don't care about, or that you don't want to do.

Make sure you start with your priority wedding pillar — if it's the venue then work from booking that first.

Remember, these are generic tasks for weddings; you don't have to have them all. Please don't think because it lists 'videographer' that you need one, because you don't. Allocate what you think should happen and when based on *your priorities*. There are plenty of wedding suppliers up and down the country that will be able to support you, from last-minute to years in advance bookings.

If your wedding dress is a priority, move it to the top of the list. Make it one of the first items you sort out. If flowers are your thing and you want to book a sought-after florist, push that up the list and move it to the top and focus on it first.

This is *your* list. Lots of people get stuck on the idea of doing things in a set order. Don't worry about this. You can spend hours and hours searching for the best wedding timelines and plans, but it might not help because it won't be personal to you and what you want.

I want you to look completely differently at the tasks that need to be done. I want you to think about what you *really* care about and do that first. Don't worry, everything will still get done, but you'll have reframed and refocused on what you care about the most.

Once you've completed this you'll have a basic framework. This is the supporting structure for your wedding planning.

The reason why you needed to get this big framework down is because it then allows you to focus on the small things, the elements of the wedding that make it yours. These are the parts you'll remember, the parts that, when weaved all together, will tell the story of your wedding day. They will be the things in ten years' time that your friends still talk about.

But we can't get there without a solid plan. So, we are outlining the big picture first. Then, through later tasks, we will explore your options, we will look at how you turn your feelings and visions into a wedding. We will look at the steps we need to take to bring it all to life.

The example below is just a guide. If you can, try and work out your order before looking at this one. Make a list of how many months there are before your wedding and start listing all the tasks that need to be completed and when.

Wedding Planning Tasks Example Timeline

Buy wedding insurance. This is the most important thing. Please do this now. Stop whatever you are doing and go and buy your insurance right now. If COVID-19 has taught us anything, it's the importance of comprehensive wedding insurance.

12 months to go:

- Plan your guest list — confirming your numbers.
- Plan and agree your final budget.
- Pick a date.
- Start your venue search.
- Research! Research! Research! Start looking for ideas.
- Choose and ask your bridal party to be part of the wedding.
- Book your venue(s).

11 months to go:

- Make a wedding website.
- Research and book a photographer.
- Meet with caterers.
- Book a wedding coordinator.
- Send save the dates.
- Book accommodation (pre-wedding/post-wedding).

10 months to go:

- Start wedding dress shopping/suit shopping.
- Book a band/DJ/sort out a music playlist.
- Confirm and book caterers and all food.
- Plan your venue decorations.
- Start making your DIY projects.
- Book a videographer.

9 months to go:

- More DIY making, searching, buying and general wedding fun!
- Order additional items you might need (chairs, tables etc.).
- Confirm flowers.
- Book your honeymoon.
- Plan for dress fittings.
- Book or sort your wedding transport.

8 months to go:

- Arrange the ceremony details.
- Buy your wedding shoes and accessories.
- Plan the legal arrangements (for civil ceremony).
- Plan your bann readings (church wedding).
- More making of DIY items.

7 months to go:

- Sort the wedding drinks (order glasses/buy alcohol/arrange paid bar details).
- Arrange the ceremony details (sort order of service/readings/hymns/music).
- Buy the bridesmaids' dresses/groomsmens' suits.
- Plan your hair and make-up trial.
- More making of the DIY items.

6 months to go:

- Make or buy the invites and send them out.
- Buy the wedding rings.
- Create your working document.
- Make a gift list plan.

5 months to go:

- Have a month off! I'm serious. Plan to take some time out from wedding planning.

4 months to go:

- You might need another dress or suit fitting.
- Confirm RSVPs. Start working on the table plan.

3 months to go:

- Confirm the table plan and chase any outstanding RSVPs.
- Attend your hen party/stag party/bridal shower.

2 months to go:

- Attend your hair and make-up trial.
- Finalise your working document and wedding setup plans.

1 month to go:

- Stop all making and 'DIY-ing'. What isn't made and finished by now will just cause too much stress.
- A final dress fitting might be needed.
- Plan for beauty treatments — facial/tanning/nails.

2 weeks to go:

- Attend wedding rehearsal (church).
- Call suppliers with any last minute changes or updates.

1 week to go:

- Chill the hell out!
- Beauty treatments — facial/tanning/nails.
- Pack an overnight bag(s).
- Check lists and your working document to ensure all items are packed and ready to go.

Questions:

- What's missing from this list for you?
- Have you ensured your priority items have been dealt with first?
- Does this timeline plan reflect your wedding vision statement?

Top Tip: One of the best things you can do for stress-free wedding planning is to set a fake end date. Trick your brain into thinking the deadline is a month before your actual wedding day. You want and need time to relax, time to switch your brain off or deal with last-minute emergencies before the wedding. A month before the big day is the time you need to start stepping away from the glue gun.

Don't let your wedding fill all the time available, because it will try to. It will push and pull and expand and squeeze into all the corners of your life. Make sure you keep it in a tight box.

ELEVEN

The Secret

The secret to creating the perfect wedding planning timeline is: there is no secret. Annoying, right?

It honestly doesn't really matter where you start and which month you buy your dress or book your photographer. There is no real right or wrong answer. There is no quick fix or magic bullet. As long as your priorities are worked on first, then everything will get done. And it will be completed in the right order.

There are so many rumours going around. There is this idea that if you don't book everything quickly, and in a panic, you will miss out. There are plenty of amazing suppliers. There are hundreds of beautiful dresses. When you are clear on your priorities, you don't feel like you've mixed up the order of what to do and when; you can relax and know the elements you care about are in the bag.

Here's an example:

You and your partner love music, so it's important to you to book the right band, but instead of focusing your search on a band, you've read you need to get your invites sent no later than ten months before your wedding. So, you focus on that for the first six weeks of your planning. That's six weeks you could have been working on what you *really* cared about! Looking for a band! You then realise the band you wanted are booked and you've got to change your planned date or find a new band!

That would be tragic. But if you'd booked your band first and focused on your priorities it might not have happened.

There are enough amazing wedding suppliers in the world and you will find what you are looking for. Not every supplier will be booked up two years in advance.

For my wedding, I went through five pizza suppliers until we found the one. I didn't end up ordering my flowers until two days before my wedding — it was fine, a tad stressful, but totally fine. The flowers looked beautiful and they were ordered from a supermarket via online shopping. No one even knew. I saved loads of money and I was really happy with the result but that's because I knew flowers weren't my priority. I knew I didn't want to spend thousands of pounds on flowers.

Your priorities are what's important; don't let the world tell you what your wedding should be like or the order you should book it in. Just use this as a guide. It doesn't really matter where you start as long as your priorities are in check.

I know I keep harping on about priorities but it's so important if you want to create a meaningful and personal wedding. If you care about your band you need to book them first, even if you haven't got a venue! Yes, you can still book a band without a venue!

There are no rules, just your personal priorities.

- We've looked at which elements of your wedding you want to make DIY.
- We've looked at the wedding pillars and you've decided which is your driver — the key element that will lead your wedding planning timeline.
- We've still got your vision statement clear and central to wedding decisions.

And when you add these all together, you create your personal wedding timeline. The secret weapon you have to ensure your wedding planning fits with your priorities.

The Secret

DIY Wedding Elements
(The items you really want to DIY – food, drink, decorations.)

+

Your Wedding Planning Pillar
(The most important thing to you; the item that leads your wedding planning journey e.g. budget/venue.)

+

Wedding Vision Statement
(The summary of what you wedding is all about.)

= Your person wedding timeline!

TWELVE

The Personal Planning Timeline

Your personal timeline is how you start to tell your wedding story. Now you have your basic framework, we need to make it special, personalised and meaningful.

How to make your wedding planning timeline more personal

I want you to add to the timeline you have created, and not just the things you 'should do'. Let's start to add the extras, *the special details*. The extra activities you want to do surrounding your wedding. Often these are the things that get forgotten.

For example:

- You might want to add monthly coffee dates with your mum and mum-in-law to keep them updated on weddings plans, helping them to feel a part of the process.
- Or you might want to add in a movie night with

your bridesmaids, watching all of the best wedding films.

- You might want to add in a monthly date night with your partner, so you can keep the marriage in the forefront of your mind and not just the wedding.

These events are just as important as choosing your invites or centrepieces. You won't get the chance to do these once you've had your wedding day, so it's important you factor them in to your wedding planning timeline now.

Your wedding doesn't have to be a one-day event. You can sprinkle in wedding activities to make it last longer and to help you enjoy the whole process. It's important that you plan these into your personal wedding planning timeline otherwise they won't happen. Time will run away with you and you'll miss out on some of the important moments of your wedding planning journey.

This is how you create your personal timeline: by adding in all the extras. Your wedding timeline should be different to everyone else's. It shouldn't be a one size fits all. You might need three months to choose your venue, but then the first dress you try on is perfect!

This is the start of a more detailed personalised plan. This is again how you make your wedding different and meaningful, because you are personalising your timeline, you are zooming out and exploring your wedding as more than just a singular event. These 'extras' are the moments you'll remember forever, make time for them.

Activity Ten

EXTRA TIMELINE DETAILS

For this activity you will need to go back through the personal wedding planning timeline you created in the last activity, then add all *additional things* you want to do under each month.

Examples could include:

- Afternoon tea with your grandma to talk about your dress.
- Attending a wedding fair with your best friend.
- Going back to a wedding dress shop and trying on wedding dresses after you've chosen yours. Trying on crazy, ugly dresses that you'd never pick! Have fun now the pressure to find the perfect one is off.
- A film night with your bridesmaids to watch wedding films and eat popcorn.
- A date night with your partner to celebrate what you are looking forward to most about getting married.
- A meal with both sides of your families leading up

to the wedding, so everyone gets to know each other.

- Add space. Plan for days in your diary where you can relax and chill out. This day, this wedding, will have a huge impact on your life, so give yourself space and time to process it.
- Schedule a spa day at home and pamper yourself.
- What else can you think of that you'd like to make time for?

Timeline pressure points

Next, go back through your timeline and start to highlight the pressure points. Underline the tasks that make you feel stressed or the parts that you are not looking forward to.

It is important you bring awareness and start conversations around these pressure points and stress triggers — because you can then start to mitigate them and you can ask for help.

For example:

If the thought of dress shopping worries you because you are conscious of your body, speak to a close friend, let them know your concerns, ask them to help, to encourage you or support you.

If you are worried about booking your venue because it's far away from where you live and you fear it will upset your family, highlight this as a stress point. Be kind to yourself and give yourself extra time to make decisions. Why not go out for a meal with your family and share some of your worries?

Let others know about the parts of the wedding planning process that are worrying you; it might surprise you how much people want to help.

Questions:

- What else could you do to ease the stress of the elements that are worrying you? Could you remove them from your wedding?
- Could you ask for help? Professional help from a wedding planner, or what about a friend? Could you delegate some tasks to your partner or a friend?

In the next section we will start to break down how to save money in each of the areas listed. So, if budgets and money are a pressure point, we will look at how you can be creative around every element of your wedding. And of course, we will look at how each of these elements fits into your vision statement, but before that you need to get to work with some more research.

THIRTEEN

Research

The more time you spend researching your wedding ideas, the easier it will be to plan and to save money.

My tipi wedding, a personal story:

I was adamant I was having a tipi wedding. That was what was on my mood board. I went to see one, I fell in love and I was sure that was exactly what my wedding would look like. I costed it up and checked the sizes and the decorations. But when I started to work through the practical actions that I needed to take, and when I tried to match the tipi with my vision statement, I just couldn't make it work. I couldn't make it squeeze into an element that really mattered to me. In the end, what I created was so much more suited to my *real* vision. Although the tipi would have *looked* like I wanted it to, it wouldn't have allowed me to have the *feel* I wanted.

But often, we can't know this without knowing how we want to feel, researching and then moving through the timeline planning process to see if it's possible to create the feelings we want.

It's only when I started to do this research, I realised a tipi wasn't fitting with how I wanted my wedding to feel. And this is what happens with so many of the couples I work with in their wedding planning journey. It's only when you dig deeper and explore how you can bring your ideas into reality that you realise what will work and what won't.

Amy's story

Amy was set on a festival wedding. She thought it would encompass the relaxed feelings she wanted, but as we talked through her ideas and researched the cost of tents and toilets and outdoor food suppliers, the truth became clearer. Amy wanted to feel free on her wedding day, she wanted her guests to have fun and she didn't want anything to feel prescriptive. Amy thought the only way to do this was with an outdoor festival wedding, the type she'd seen on Pinterest. Yet together we talked about the places she loved and what made her happy, and really it was a destination wedding. A ceremony on the beach, with the sand between her toes and not a Portaloo in sight. She'd got lost and drifted from the feelings she really wanted to experience. She didn't want to cater for guests for a whole weekend, she just wanted them to feel relaxed and there were other ways to achieve this.

This is why you need to research.

You might think research should have been covered sooner. The truth is, you won't have stopped researching throughout this whole process of planning your wedding.

But if you start with too much research, your priorities will get knocked off the top spot.

- You'll focus on searching for things that don't even make your list of top ten priorities.
- You'll get distracted by ideas or inspired by wedding fairs.
- You'll be lulled into suggestions from others.
- You'll be pulled in all directions.

However, once you've narrowed down what's important to you, you can then start valuable research, research with purpose and specificity.

How to research

The best research you can do is to talk to other brides and grooms. You can learn so much. It's not copying, it is sharing, and it lets ideas build. You take an idea that you hear from someone else and you can add the '*you-ness*' and unique personality you have. You can add your life experiences and the things you love, and it changes it totally!

Other brides and grooms can help by sharing their experiences too. Things that wished they had or hadn't done. They can share perspective on what matters and what doesn't.

Research as much as you can in all of the areas of your wedding that you have identified as a priority. From now on in you need to carry out research like it's your job.

Start a folder, a physical folder, and pick up all the items you love: cards, pictures, flower names, your partner's favourite band's CD cover. Collect things that make you happy and help describe who you are — words, gifts, food, songs. Have fun and go crazy. This is your 'swipe file' or wedding journal. It's a collection of images, themes, words and ideas that will help you design your wedding based on the ideas and elements that inspire you and catch your attention. Use this to jot down ideas as soon as they come to mind, even if they aren't fully formed yet. This is how you'll really add your personality to your wedding.

Where to conduct research:

- **Other people's weddings!** One of the best places to conduct research is at other people's weddings. Take notes and think about the parts that you loved, the parts that flowed and felt good. Think about how you felt at different points. One of the most popular wedding complaints is that guests felt hungry! Think about other weddings you've been to and how you felt throughout. What parts could you take and make your own?

- **Pinterest** (with caution). I love Pinterest. I've got so many different boards for all the lives I've imagined I'll live and all the holidays I'll never take. But weddings and Pinterest have got tangled and intertwined into a list of 'must haves' instead of a place for ideas. Use Pinterest for research, but with caution. Take an idea that you love on Pinterest and try and make it personal. Look at the idea and check if it fits with your wedding vision statement. Change the idea slightly; don't worry about getting it exactly the same, make it yours. You don't want a carbon copy wedding, so don't just copy ideas from Pinterest, make them yours. Mix two ideas together. Make Pinterest ideas your own.

- **Magazines**. Every month in the lead-up to my wedding, I bought a wedding magazine and I took myself out for coffee and cake and read the magazine front to back. I used the magazine as a time for myself to enjoy the wedding planning process. You can get so many ideas from magazines. It doesn't just have to been wedding magazines either, craft magazines and mindfulness magazines have lots of wonderful ideas. But use these ideas as your starting points, let them influence you but don't let them become a checklist.

- **Instagram.** Find wedding accounts you love, wedding planners you like or just use hashtags to search. You will find a gold mine of other people's wedding ideas. Ideas and pictures will allow you to steal displays and look at DIY creations in a new light. Hashtags to search: **#diyweddingdecor #diyweddingideas #diywedding.**

- **Blog posts and venue websites/social media pages.** Recommended suppliers on venue websites are a great place to start when researching. It can mean the supplier has some experience and real-life recommendations behind them, it can also mean they know your venue inside out, which is a real bonus. You might also be able to look at real pictures from a wedding or even get in touch with other couples that have used the supplier and ask for a recommendation. Facebook has honest and relevant reviews; it can be a good place to research if a supplier is for you or not.

- **Books.** There are so many fantastic wedding planning books and guides, planners and task lists that can help you research ideas and places to find suppliers.

But for me the most important thing you can do for research is to look at your life. What do you love? What sums you up? What makes you, you? What about your partner? How can you bring these elements into your wedding?

Stick a picture of yourself and your partner in the middle of a piece of paper. Around it draw the words, ideas and even pictures that would help describe you both. List the things you love. The places you've been. How could you fit some of those into your wedding? How could you research these ideas further? How could you turn this into an element at your wedding? Your wedding is about you. You are the best possible piece of research for your wedding.

Use your life as inspiration for your wedding; that's how you'll make it personal, memorable and meaningful.

Part Two Summary

We have covered a lot of content in this section. This is your planning framework, and it's the structure you will use to form the base of all your wedding planning and timeline work from now on.

To summarise this section, you now have:

- Looked at what your next steps are in relation to your priorities and your wedding vision statement.
- A clear step-by-step timeline for your wedding planning journey and you know what tasks need to be completed and by when. You'll keep adding to this, but the good news is you've started to make it personal.
- Ideas to start researching.

In the next section we are going to add even more detail to these plans, because it's the details that matter.

Activity Eleven

Before moving on to the next section make sure you have confirmed your wedding planning timeline. Add lots of the extras we talked about too. Make sure you know where the pressure points are and then start to list how you can deal with those pressures.

Print your timeline off and stick it somewhere you'll see it every day in your house. Action relieves anxiety, so when you can see your plans are in place, when you know that everything is scheduled to be completed at some point in the future, it will help you relax and enjoy your wedding planning.

The planning timeline is the hardest part of the wedding planning process. Once you've completed it, you can dive into even more detailed plans and start to make your wedding look pretty!

You will also need to start thinking about your budget. Speak with your partner and have a good estimate, a strong idea of what you will be working towards. Be realistic and don't rush the discussion. We will cover budget more in the next section, but start the discussions early.

Finally, you will need to get stuck into your research! Start exploring all of your ideas and options. Why not make an element or design part of your wedding that would reflect you and your partner? Like a mock invite or a centrepiece? Have fun with it.

Part Three – Making Plans

FOURTEEN

Let's Talk Money

Budget.

You might not want to talk about the wedding budget or saving money. It feels so boring, oppressive and restricting, but you can make it fun, I promise. You need to keep your personal priorities in mind and not let the world (or any bossy relatives) tell you where your money should or shouldn't go.

A recent Hitched.co.uk article found the average cost of a wedding in the UK (in 2019) was an eye-watering £31,974[1]. Money can cause a lot of stress and anxiety. There are hidden pressures, and traditional expectations can often rear their ugly heads. Getting married shouldn't be about debt, it's about your commitment to each other. That's why this book is focused on feelings and priorities, they're all that matter. Your wedding doesn't have to cost a fortune to be meaningful or memorable.

If you want the designer dress, that is absolutely fine. If it takes 50% of your budget that is absolutely fine too, it just means you need to adjust everything else. It might mean you're wearing the dress in your parents' garden or at the local village hall, but if that's the dress you want and that is your priority, you can make it work. It's all about balance. And garden weddings are beautiful.

But, you've got to have a serious talk about budgets with your partner. Why don't you go out for a drink, or host a meeting at your kitchen table? Make sure you are both in agreement about your budget.

Tips for talking about budget

- Plan a time to talk budgets; don't just spring it on your partner. Set some time aside, turn off the TV, put down your phones and make space for an honest conversation.
- Be realistic. Don't stretch yourselves so much that the year leading up to your wedding makes you feel miserable because you're living off pasta to try and save money!
- Check that you are both really happy with what you are planning on spending. Be honest with each other.
- Remind yourselves of your priorities list and focus on budgeting for those items first.
- Plan regular budget meetings so you can keep on top of your expenses.
- Don't put off talking about money. Some of the most beautiful weddings cost the least amount of money. It doesn't matter what your budget is, what matters most is that you have a budget and a plan and that you and your partner agree and are happy with it.

When it comes to deciding on your budget I think it's best to keep it simple. You've got two options here:

1. Plan the wedding of your dreams at whatever
the cost.

Then work out how much you need to save to make it happen. Calculate how much you can save per month and then work out how many months you will have to save for to reach the planned target.

With this option you make no compromises on the wedding you want, other than it might take you five years to get there. But everything about a DIY wedding is about compromise and balance, and that's why we focused on your priorities and motivations. It's okay to have everything you want and just delay your wedding until you can afford to pay for it rather than starting married life with debt.

Or,

2. Figure out when you want to get married.
Calculate how much you can realistically save in
that time. That's your budget. Simple.

No loans, no pushing yourself to the limit. You plan, you save, you have a wonderful wedding sooner rather than later.

I can hear you telling me: *"How can we plan our budget when we don't know how much venues or flowers are?"*

I would encourage you to consider your budget *before* doing extensive research into venues and flowers, especially if budget is your wedding pillar. Weddings can spiral in costs, and it's really not worth getting into debt to have the wedding of your dreams. For some people, you might need to do more research before you can say definitively "this is our budget". However, you can make your wedding beautiful whatever your budget, so don't let your research dictate your spending. You decide what you want to spend based on what you can afford and save for, and then you make your suppliers and choices fit with that limit. Planning your budget this way round forces you to stick to your plans, otherwise you're letting the wedding industry dictate what your wedding should cost.

£5,000 Budget

£10,000 Budget

£20,000 Budget

You can make them all work.

When you know what you really care about, when you know how *you* want to feel and how you want *your wedding* to feel, you can let go of so many elements that you don't need. You can stop spending money on the things you think you 'should' have.

Priorities again.

We are reframing how we look at weddings, and it is really hard. There is a whole industry built around telling you what you should and shouldn't have and it's powerful. Don't lose sight of your original goal. Your budget can support your vision statement. You just might have to be really tough on some areas and make some compromises. Nobody likes the thought of compromise when talking about weddings. But it's not really a compromise, it's more a clarification of how you want your wedding to be, a focus on priorities. Instead of spending lots of money on what you're told you should spend it on, like a three-course roast dinner and a string quartet, be clear and know what you want and spend your money accordingly.

Activity Twelve

THE BUDGET BREAKDOWN

Below is a list of the standard wedding expense areas. These are the key areas we listed in the wedding planning timeline activity. Remember that these are only standard budget items and you don't need to budget for them all if they aren't your priorities. Don't feel like you need them, but have a think about what percentage of your budget you would like to allocate to each area if you want them as part of your wedding. Add any areas you think are missing.

Remember to take into account:

- Your wedding vision statement
- Your priorities.

Go through each item and estimate (roughly) the amount of money or the percentage of your budget that you would like to allocate to each area. Don't worry too much for now about it being accurate, it's just a rough plan to get you started. If you know certain areas are your priority go ahead and add more money on that section.

Don't be shy.

If you want those Louboutin shoes, go for it. Just be prepared to compromise on your photobooth or evening bar.

Once you've split the money out into the sections it gives you a rough idea of the areas where you might need to inject a bit more creativity (to save money) or the areas where you might need to add a few more DIY elements to help with costs.

VENUE:

Ceremony

Reception

Overnight accommodation

Celebrant/church

Equipment hire

CATERING:

Food

Drinks

Cake

CLOTHING:

Suit

Wedding dress

Bridesmaids' dresses

Groomsmen

DECORATIONS:

Flowers

Venue styling

Stationery

TRANSPORT

OTHER:

Music/band

Hair & make-up

Wedding coordinator

Gifts

Photographer

Videographer

Rings

Stag/hen party

Contingency

FIFTEEN

Refining the Details

It's time to talk about the details. You can make beautiful decorations and have wonderful ideas, but unless you have an even more beautiful plan nobody is going to see them.

There is only one way to get a smooth-running, carefree wedding, and that is to put hours and hours and hours of work into the planning.

You see, it can be hectic, messy and busy when the DIY wedding setup is in full force. Without a detailed plan, the ideas you sweated over, well I hate to say it, but they get left on the back burner.

Let me tell you a story.

It's a story that I've seen time and time again. As a wedding coordinator, I often turn up to a DIY wedding setup and I see piles and piles of unopened Amazon Prime boxes. It makes me shudder. Napkins are mixed with plastic cups and bunting. The special twine you ordered is hidden under a blow-up microphone and a cake slice.

Carnage begins when a bridesmaid is tasked to find the glitter pegs ordered twelve months ago because the photo wall needs to be set up. Fights break out over who's got the scissors. The hunt for sticky tape takes hours, then someone dares to ask for Blutack...

It makes me feel stressed just thinking about it. But worse than this, I've seen craft projects that lovely brides have spent months making sit in unopened boxes under a cake table because no one knew 'where they were supposed to go' or they didn't know how to set them up. I've known brides stay up until 3am (3am!) the night before their wedding hanging the last few decorations.

Tucked up in bed is where you should be at 3am on your pre-wedding night (unless of course you want a roaring party before you say "I do"), but definitely not hanging decorations and climbing ladders. I'm pretty sure that is what they call *asking for trouble*.

I've been knee-deep in a wedding when a bridesmaid has bounded up to me, sweaty and panicked:

> "Where are the cake boxes! The bride has specifically asked for the cake to be boxed up and not served on plates, but we've been searching high and low and we can't find them..."

> "Stop, breathe."

The poor bridesmaid has wasted over an hour of dancing time searching high and low for cake boxes. And the bride, by the looks of her in that moment, couldn't care less.

I don't want your wedding to be like this. So let's learn how to make detailed plans and then you can sleep soundly with all the Prime boxes tucked neatly in the recycling bin months before the big day.

The aim is for you to have a DIY wedding so well-planned it looks like everything happened by accident, as if it was such a coincidence that the day flowed so well. Plan so hard to make it look like there isn't a plan. That's the goal. You've done lots of this work with your detailed wedding planning timeline, but let's add more specific detail.

This is my aim for all of the events I manage. It is one of the hardest parts of event management. Often, it is the most boring part too, but I promise if you miss this stage, your wedding day will have holes. You will make everything twice as hard, and possibly spend more money than you need. You will stress out your suppliers too. A calm bride is a well-planned and super-organised bride (or groom).

More research

We started to look at research in part two, but as we've explored further, budget and research are so closely linked you will need to be moving from one to the other, checking in with your budget and conducting more research if the current ideas aren't fitting into the financial plans.

Most people fall into the trap of their wedding looking good but not planning the details and not planning the experience for their guests. Don't fall for that.

The details matter to you. However, often guests won't notice these elements, but what they do notice is how it all comes together. They see the big picture and they feel the overall experience you have created. But you can't create a big picture without thousands of little details. You need to start working away at these details as they will all add up and feed into the big picture.

How do you ensure you are working towards the big picture?

This is where I want to talk about a different kind of research. I don't mean a Google here and there, or an evening spent on Pinterest. This is the type of research that will make your wedding different and unique. This type of research is time-consuming. Most people won't bother with it. But this type of research can be a game changer, if you let it.

This is what we call refining the details.

This type of research is used to break down every single wedding element and look at it through a microscope, examining every single task on your planning timeline and then turning them into more personal and bespoke wedding elements. You need to start drilling down to the details of your wedding.

This is how you now move forward with your timeline plans.

This is how you start to build the big picture:

You break your wedding down into the smallest of pieces, the tiniest of details, to then build it up. The details make the big picture. This is why they matter. You need to break all of your wedding elements down to their bare bones, then research all of them as separate elements and ideas and bring them back together again.

You need to do this for every single element of your wedding. Don't skip anything! This will take a lot of time, but in the end, I promise it will save you time.

Let me explain.

This can be one of the trickiest and most boring parts of wedding planning. If you do this well, you will be ecstatic with the finished product of your wedding. You will have examined every element and each part will represent you. There won't be anything that you'd have done differently, no regrets.

This is how you will make your wedding unique.

If you want to have a wedding with no regrets you need to consider every element in excruciating detail. It means when someone 'helpfully' suggests you 'should' have something, you can *know* that you've considered everything in detail, and you are more than happy with your choices.

I'm going to show you how to break down all the elements of your wedding but first, I want to share a personal story with you.

My wedding cake, a personal story:

Wedding cakes. Honestly, I wasn't bothered about spending £900 on a cake. Firstly, because I'm allergic to dairy and I was pretty sure I wouldn't even be able to buy a nice cake that I could eat and wouldn't cost a fortune. Secondly, because we had decided to have our wedding cake for dessert, I wanted people to it eat it rather than it get thrown away and forgotten about after the main meal. Just a nice extra that everyone just looked at.

Think about it: a lot of people go on their honeymoon straight after their wedding, so what are you going to do with half a leftover wedding cake? Anyway. I really wanted someone special to me to make the cake. That was part of my wedding *feeling*. I wanted family and close friends to feel a part of our wedding, and what better way than making our wedding cake? The idea that they could be so central to our wedding still makes me emotional today; someone took the time and energy to actually make our wedding cake! I knew seeing the cake they had lovingly made on my wedding day would mean so much more. I would get so much more joy from that than seeing a shop-bought cake.

This meant the cake also fitted into our budget and it meant I had very little to do around sorting and sourcing it. Another item I could tick off the wedding to-do list with very little stress.

To me, this wedding cake was more than a cake, it was a symbol of love in action (one of the themes of my wedding). If I hadn't broken down the 'wedding cake' element of our wedding and explored and researched all the options available to me, I wouldn't have realised how it meant more to me to have this wonderful *feeling* surrounding my wedding cake rather than what it looked like. Unless I'd broken down my wedding planning timeline and list and really explored where my priorities were, I would have just bought a cake. I wouldn't have made it special and different and unique.

How can you break down a wedding element or a job on your to-do list?

For each element of your wedding you will need to assess it against four key areas:

1. **Feelings** – Ask yourself if this element of the wedding is focused on the overall feeling you want to create for your day? How can you make it fit

with your wedding vision statement? Is it an extra, or does it add to the feeling you want to create?

2. **Creativity/DIY** – How can you make this element of your wedding more creative? More unique? How can you make it different? Do you want to DIY it? How can you make this element reflect you and your partner?

3. **Budget** – Can you assess if this element of your wedding fits with your budget? Do you really need it? Is it a priority? How could you make it cheaper? Does it fit with the amount of money you have allocated to it?

4. **Actions** – What actions or further jobs has this one element created? List every single task that needs to be completed as part of this wedding element. This is effectively a really detailed list for that one element on the wedding planning timeline.

Let's talk through some examples, as this type of research might seem confusing or complicated. It's necessary to save stress and create detailed plans.

For example:

Let's talk through wedding invitations. This might be something that has appeared early on your timeline as a task you might need to complete fairly soon. It's a good place to start as an example to break down.

Wedding Invitation Research Breakdown:

1. Feelings

What on earth do wedding invites have to do with feelings? How can they create a feeling? Let's say some of the feelings you wanted to create as part of your wedding were:

"family focused and full of love"

How do you want this represented in your invite?

You could look at the words you might use in the invite, or the overall design. Could you have a 'colour your own invite' so it really shows off that family feel? What next? Think about every element surrounding the invite. You might want to send them all via post, as it feels personal and another example of love. Each one has been addressed and carried to the post office by hand.

How do you want to feel when you look back at your invitations? That's a *feeling* element too. Do you want to remember making them with your bridesmaids or your fiancé? Do you want to remember how you sipped prosecco and watched films as you stuffed envelopes, or do you want it to be a solitary task you worked on steadfastly over a summer while you stayed at home and saved for your wedding?

How do you want guests to feel when they open your invite? Or are you not really bothered about that feeling, because they've got the information they need, and all you really care about is them being there on the day? It doesn't matter what your answers are, as long as you've considered everything surrounding *feelings* in this one element of your wedding.

2. Creativity/DIY

Next you need to examine the element and decide if you want it to be DIY. Do you want to make the invites yourself? Or are you happy to just get it done and ticked off your list as quickly as possible? You could print some beautiful invites off Vistaprint and then be done with that wedding element.

You then need to examine this element for creativity too. How could you make your invites different and unique? Go crazy on Pinterest and Google, look in magazines, soak up ideas, write them all down, colours, themes and images. Write down all these ideas. They will help you tie it all together and it will help you decide how you could create your own spin on some unique invites.

3. Budget

How much will the invites cost to make? Are they your priority? Do you need them? Do they fit into your vision statement? How can you make them cheaper? What about e-invites? Or a Facebook group even? If it's not a priority for you, and you want to save money, then don't worry about fancy invites. What could you make yourself? Think carefully. Do you really want to spend money on this item?

If you have allocated a set budget for invites and, for you, they are a priority — they are, after all, the first thing your guests will see and they can often set the tone for your wedding — then enjoy making them or buying them. Let it be a fun part of your wedding. But make sure you plan and stick to your budget.

4. Actions

The next step in refining research and breaking elements down is to list every single action that needs to be completed for your invitation task to be fully finished. Your list of actions should be really comprehensive and detailed. It will feel like a lot, but it actually makes planning easier, as you've broken down one task into smaller bite-size chunks.

Invites actions list:

- Research invite designs.
- Research the cheapest shops for the materials.
- Book time in your diary to make the invites with your bridesmaids.
- Design the content for inside the invite with your partner.
- Calculate the cost of postage and check this against your budget. Do you need to post all the invites?
- Complete a test postage run. Does it just need one stamp?
- Decide on a date for your invites to be sent out.
- Make a prototype of your invite.
- Order glue, scissors and the other materials you need to create invites.
- Check planned costs against your budget again and adjust accordingly.
- Make invites.
- Post invites.

By breaking down the wedding element and assessing it against the research questions, you end up being really happy with all the decisions you make. It also makes each component personal and ensures it's been carefully considered. Plus, it makes tasks seem achievable.

Let's explore this process for the photography element of your wedding too.

Photography Research Breakdown:

1. Feelings

You might want photography to feel like a small part of your day, as you might hate having your picture taken. You might feel like you want candid, intimate shots. Or you might not be too worried about lots of formal photos. You could even decide not to have a group shot after the ceremony. You could even decide you don't want to have a 'formal' photographer, because of how all of this makes you feel.

Think about how you want to feel in relation to your photographs Do you want timeless and elegant? Do you want them to be over as quickly as possible? Or do you want to have lots of fun, silly snaps? How do you want to feel? Pick a photographer based on this.

2. Creativity/DIY

Could a friend take your wedding pictures? Photography could be a part of your wedding that you decide to DIY. Or you could want some really fun and creative shots from the day. How could you make photography at your wedding different and unique? Could you have disposable cameras on each table at the wedding breakfast?

3. Budget

Could you buy a nice mid-range camera and get a trusted friend to be assigned to taking photos? You could list all the shots you want them to take. Then you could even sell the camera afterwards? It would make it cheaper and you'd still get great photos. Or hire a photographer for half a day and get a friend to do the evening shots? There are lots of options to help you save money on photography.

4. Actions

Next you need to list all the actions that surround your photography decisions. These could be:

- Research the best camera in your budget.
- Buy the camera.
- Allocate a friend to take pictures.
- Have a practice 'pre-wedding' shoot.
- Plan how the pictures will be backed up and saved.
- Create a backup plan, just in case.
- Create a list of pictures you would like your friend to take.
- Sell the camera after wedding.

You need to complete this breakdown for everything on your wedding timeline list, even though it feels like a lot. You'll be surprised what matters more to you.

Remember this breakdown will vary depending on your priorities. Some items might take a while to break down, while others you might be able to skip right past.

I understand this can seem daunting. Breaking down every element in this way can feel like a lot, but it's the only way to truly ensure you are happy with all your decisions. It allows you to consider everything. You'll find you come across some elements and realise how much they really don't matter to you, and that's great. You won't even need to go through all four key questions, because you'll know it's not a priority.

Once you have created the detailed action plan list for every single element of your wedding, you can then turn it into a checklist and add each task to the appropriate month on your timeline. Then you can really start to formalise your plans and start ticking things off the list!

SIXTEEN

The DIY Wedding Setup

Your action plans should now be bursting at the seams with bite-sized jobs to complete. The more you do now, the more you'll enjoy your big day and the setup surrounding it.

It's time to start thinking about the practicalities of your plans and the wedding day set up.

More often than not, with DIY weddings, you will be able to access your venue before the morning of the big day. This is great, as it gives you time to plan and prepare your venue. But you don't have as much time as you think. This is why you need to be organised. You need detailed plans showing exactly how your venue needs to be set up.

The setup of a DIY wedding is almost my favourite part. There is excitement in the air. A buzz. You can feel the emotion dripping off every person. The anticipation and weight of the commitment two people are about to make is electric. But time and time again I've seen couples so lost in the mess of disorganisation that they miss these moments. They miss the build-up.

I don't want that for you. I want your wedding setup to be fun. There have been times where I've seen wonderfully crafted DIY projects left behind tables or set up in haste. If you've spent twelve months working on decorations you want your guests to see them; you don't want to run out of time. This is why your setup plans are so important.

Setting up your venue

Imagine:

The day before your wedding is finally here.

You wake up tired but excited. You know there is a lot to do, but you are looking forward to it. You have a clear plan and you know which tasks can be easily delegated and managed.

Arriving at your venue, you smile. Trusted friends are ready and raring to go. They know what they need to do to get the wedding setup. They don't have many questions because your plans are so clear.

This is the dream. This is the plan to make wedding setup fun!

When you've created action lists for all of the elements on your wedding planning timeline, it's easy to see what needs to be done in advance. But you also need to create action lists for all of the DIY elements you want to set up on your big day so the dream we discussed above can become a reality.

This could be items like a photobooth, decorative 'stations', a DIY bar or even your guest book table. Whatever items need to be set up at your venue, each needs a detailed action plan of *how* they should be set up and where.

This is for a number of reasons:

1. It means the idea is out of your head and on paper. Anyone could help set it up if for some reason you couldn't.
2. It lets you work out how long something might take to set up, meaning you can plan and work out how long it will take you to set up the whole venue. You don't want to run out of time.
3. It means you don't forget anything or miss anything off your list of items to bring to the venue.

For example:

You would create a master list on an Excel document or on paper called 'DIY setup'. Here you would list all the elements that needed to be set up and break them down, like in the example on the following page.

I'll use a random decorative prop element as an example. You might have lots of ideas for decorations like this and you need to consider how long they'll take to set up. This is an example of how detailed the setup plans need to be to allow to you to have a stress-free wedding setup. For each prop you need to list, the items/equipment required, the actions that need to be taken to 'set up' the item, where the item will be located and which boxes the equipment will be stored in.

DIY element - A decorative prop: polaroid guest book

You've decided you want to capture the faces of you guests along with their words in your guest book. So you need to list all the items and actions that must be completed to set up this particular DIY element.

Items Required:

- Guest book prop
- Table/dresser
- Polaroid camera
- Spare batteries
- Camera film
- Pens
- Guest book
- Flowers
- Vase
- Spare pens
- Table cloth
- Pegs
- String for hanging pictures

Actions to be completed:

1. Set up table/dresser.
2. Place jars, vase and flowers.
3. Display guest book, pens, camera.
4. Add spare film and batteries to storage box under table.
5. Show a bridesmaid how to change the film.

Location of equipment: Box 3 of 12.

Location of item at the wedding: To be set up by front doors of marquee.

You need to do this breakdown for every element that requires setting up at your venue. It needs to be so detailed someone else could set it up. You can even add photos of how it should look when it's finished.

This is a small example of one element that I've broken down as an example. I want to stress you will need to spend a lot of time on every DIY decoration element and break it down in this way to make your wedding setup stress-free.

However, the advantages of this work mean your wedding vision can be set up by a helpful friend or a wedding coordinator. You don't need to worry about something being missed or someone setting it up incorrectly. You'll be able to enjoy the pre-wedding setup.

Top Tip – Put all setup items in boxes and label each box. Keep an inventory of what is in each box and put a location of where the box needs to be dropped off ready for the items inside to be set up.

SEVENTEEN

Your Wedding Bible

A working document is an event management tool that is used to hold all of the details of an event. You need one too, and it's going to become your 'Wedding Bible'. A working document is any event manager's guidebook, their go-to toolkit. It is the item that we would protect with our lives.

Put really simply, a working document is a collection of all the essential documents and information you need for your wedding to run, but it's the detail it contains that is so important. It doesn't sound as flashy as a 'Wedding Bible', but it's your go-to place for storing all your plans, information and detail.

There are so many reasons why you need a working document. You need all your actions and plans listed in such detail that someone else could take your folder and run your wedding exactly as you planned. This is for a few reasons:

1. You don't know what could happen. You could get ill, break your arm, get a job promotion and run out of time to plan. You need everything out of your head and on paper. You need to be able to let someone else pick this folder up and know exactly where you are up to with your wedding planning.

2. It also helps you stay organised. If you start to get overwhelmed, you know exactly how to delegate, because everything that needs to be done will be listed, and you can keep track of who you have allocated tasks to.

3. As you get closer to the wedding, you will need to see that all the jobs have been ticked off and you will need to start loosening control. This document gives you the confidence to know you have all of your information in one place and allows you to keep track of decisions, budgets, dates for equipment deliveries and agreements with suppliers.

4. If you do decide to have an on-the-day wedding coordinator, you can then pass all of this information on to them and they can then run the show. If you don't have an on-the-day wedding coordinator, you can also pass the information on to a friend or bridesmaid to run the wedding and it's one less thing for you to worry about.

Items that need to be included in your working document:

- A full wedding schedule — including a few days before and after, showing every planned action.
- A full wedding day timeline (in excruciating detail).
- A wedding day timeline that you would share with guests, showing only relevant details.
- A list of your DIY setup items.
- A setup tasks list showing what needs to be done and when.
- All of your suppliers' contact details.
- All of the bridal party contact details.
- Emergency contacts — this could be contacts for the venue, or even emergency taxi numbers etc.
- Packing lists — one for the wedding setup, one for the night before the wedding and the night after the wedding.
- Your Doom List (don't worry, we cover this in part four).
- Directions to venues (if using multiple venues).

When you are compiling your working document, you are looking at the tasks that need to happen the week of your wedding, not just on the day. This working document is going to take you a long time to pull together, but it will be worth it. It will keep you organised and your wedding will run smoothly. It's also a great place to put your wedding vision statement to help you remember the 'real reason' for all this planning.

EIGHTEEN

Your Wedding Day

Another key item you need to add into your working document is the timeline for the wedding day. This is different from your wedding planning timeline (the list of tasks you need to complete each month before the wedding). This is the detailed plan for exactly what will happen and when on your actual wedding day.

This is one of the key tasks you need to work at getting right, because this allows you to get the flow and the *feeling* of your wedding day just right for you and your guests.

There are no quick fixes. You could copy someone else's wedding day timeline, but to make your wedding different and unique you *really* need to think about how *you* want your day to feel and how you want your *guests* to feel. Yes, we are still talking about feelings!

For example, if you want your wedding day to feel sophisticated and intimate, you might just have an afternoon tea reception and scrap the evening party. This would mean your timeline would look very different to an all-day wedding!

Questions:

- What do you remember from weddings you've been to before about the flow of the day? Did you feel bored? Or hungry? Or thirsty? How could you counter this with your wedding timeline?
- Do you want a long wedding day? Or would you rather have time to relax in the morning and take your time getting ready?

Top tips for creating a wedding day that flows

1. Treat your wedding as a normal day.

This might sound crazy, but imagine a normal day and think about when you would *normally* eat and drink. Make sure your guests are fed and watered at similar times to when they might be on a normal day. Just because it's your wedding day doesn't mean guests can skip lunch and not eat until 5pm! Even if you provide snacks and a drinks reception as an interim, it all helps guests to feel looked after. There is nothing worse than an open bar and hungry guests.

2. Create space in your timeline to allow guests to talk and mingle.

There is no need to rush. If you do have gaps in time, try and plan activities as an option for some guests. For example, if you've got lots of children attending, why not leave out garden games or indoor games? Things like a guest book or a photobooth can also be good time-fillers. But only have them if you want them; don't have extras for the sake of filling time. Wedding guests expect space and time to relax.

Remember, there are naturally lulls in time and that's okay. If your guests have been moved from a ceremony venue to another room or location, they are glad for the break. Or you can ensure there are activities to do. These don't have to cost money. Go back to your vision statement and remember the things you really want. How can you incorporate these to create flow in your wedding day?

For example:

Some weddings have long speeches with coffee and cake, whereas others 'get the speeches over with'. You can play around with the pace of your day. Fast and slow elements.

3. Finally, it's really important that you tell your guests what's going on.

You could put a timeline on your wedding website (if you have one), you could have a plan for the day in the order of service, or you could put some posters up in your reception venue. Your guests won't mind what the plan is, as long as they know what it is. This is great if your guests have got kids and need to change or feed them. Or it can be useful if you've had guests that have travelled a long way and might want to nip out to the hotel to check in. As long as your guests know the plan, they can make the most out of your day too.

Creating a wedding that flows is all about including your feelings into the timeline of the wedding day. If you want relaxed and informal, let guests know that. Play music, put blankets on chairs and let them help themselves to drinks. You set the tone by the way your day unfolds, so make sure you've thought about it.

Part Three Summary

You can't plan too much, and the more you do now, even if it seems like it would be a simple or a 'quick job' that doesn't really need planning, the better. You'll be surprised how much these quick jobs can add up! Suddenly you'll realise how much you have to do.

Plan now. Enjoy later.

To sum up this section:

- You have ensured you are talking about your budget and working to plan around it. Use research and creativity to ensure you stay on track.
- You have explored what a working document is, and you have an understanding as to why it is so important for a DIY wedding.
- You have explored why it is important to create a wedding day that flows.

Activity Thirteen

Map out your dream wedding day timeline.

Start with your highlights, the things you are really looking forward to. Plan those parts first!

Then think about your energy; you don't want to be exhausted or drained when you get to the parts you are looking forward to the most.

If you don't plan it, it won't happen. Schedule in every detail that you want to experience.

This homework should be fun! Take your time and play around with different scenarios. Try some different formats and ceremony times and see if that works for you. Don't think you have to get married at 12pm just because that's what the Royals do!

Questions:

- Have you thought about getting married in the evening? You could have a 5pm ceremony and just have an evening reception?
- What about having a lunchtime wedding and then everyone meets up again in the evening? You could have an intimate wedding breakfast with your close relatives inbetween?
- What about your energy? Have you planned time to rest?
- Have you scheduled time with a parent or time for fun photos with your bridesmaids?

No one wants a militant schedule on their wedding day, but if you don't plan your day out exactly how you want it to be, it will just happen and you'll get swept up in the moment.

Within your planning you can factor in rest time and moments of pause. This allows your day to flow and it makes sure the planning doesn't come across militant or formalised.

Top Tip – Make sure you share a peeled-back version of the wedding timeline with your guests. It's important they know what's going on. They can then help the day to stay on track too.

Part Four – What Happens if it Goes Wrong?

NINETEEN

The Doom List

Most people don't really like to talk about what could go wrong on your wedding day. It's much easier to focus on the glitter and the excitement, but I wanted to allocate a whole section of this book to look at what could go wrong. I believe if you look at all eventualities you will have more control over the outcomes as you can prepare to take action. Hopefully this will:

1. Prevent problems from happening as much as feasibly possible.
2. Mean you'll be prepared and have planned for all eventualities.
3. Minimise worry if your day doesn't go to plan.

Things can go wrong and it's important you make a plan for this. I hope everything goes perfectly on your wedding day, but all you can do is be prepared. Ultimately, if you end up married, it has been a successful day. This is the most important thing.

Planning a DIY wedding can mean you are on your own, unless you have a wedding coordinator or on-the-day wedding planner, you are responsible for pulling everything together, working with suppliers and directing the day. This is where your working document will come into its own. It will hold all of the necessary information so one of your loved ones can take control and you can sit back and enjoy the day.

There's lots you can do to prevent some of the common DIY wedding mistakes and blunders from happening at your wedding. So, let's talk about the Doom List.

This is a tool that I use for every event I manage. I've called it the Doom List, which sounds very dramatic, but it's saved me so much stress over the years.

What is a Doom List?

These are detailed documents that look at all of the 'risks' within your event. This is a list of every possible thing that could go wrong at your event, and then most importantly what you would or could do about it. But this isn't like a risk assessment in the traditional sense.

Although a Doom List sounds scary, it allows you take control. You can mitigate problems before they happen, and you can prepare for the worst-case scenario. So, if it does happen, it's not the worst thing possible, because you've already planned for it. For example, a supplier not turning up or an unexpected power cut. A Doom List is a bit like a contingency plan.

Reasons why you need a Doom List:

- **They avoid a lot of stress**. This is a document personalised to your wedding. Its objective is to solve problems that might happen on your wedding day, at your venue or with your suppliers. It can prevent a lot of stress by listing potential problems and possible solutions ahead of time. Therefore, if a problem does crop up, you've already got a plan to solve it.

- **Everyone is clear on the plan.** All staff and suppliers working on your wedding should be given a copy of this document. It means everyone knows how to deal with problems if they arise, saving time and panic should things go wrong.

- **Problems are less likely to happen**. By planning solutions for potential problems, chances are things will be less likely to go wrong. You will have spotted potential pitfalls early and you will have acted on weaker areas of your wedding planning.

- **You will feel more confident and in control**. Once you've taken time to look at what could go wrong, you will feel more confident knowing you are prepared for the worst-case scenario. Things are never as bad as you imagine anyway and more often than not, the bride and groom are enjoying their day so much they don't notice anything that doesn't go to plan.

How to make your Doom List

Making a Doom List is actually a lot simpler than it might first appear. It can also be fun, if you let it. Try not to worry; most of the time everything will go perfectly to plan. With a Doom List you are being proactive and prepared, and that's the most important thing.

Step 1 – Break your wedding into sections (an example is below). Keep in mind your sections will look different and will depend on what sort of wedding you are planning:

- Pre-Wedding
- Ceremony
- Wedding Breakfast
- Evening Reception
- Closedown.

Step 2 – For each section of your wedding, list as many things as you can that might go wrong. Be as creative, crazy and far-fetched as you can.

Step 3 – Start to create solutions to the problems that you have created. Think logically and sensibly. How might you solve these problems? What could you plan now to ease a problematic situation later? Could you create a 'Plan B' for some elements?

Step 4 – Add the solutions to the problems to create your full Doom List. Then, add this to your working document. It can be as simple as a table with three columns:

1st Column – Doom List problem.
2nd Column – Solution to problem.
3rd Column – Person in charge.

Whilst you can't solve every problem, or prepare for every possible scenario, spending some time thinking about how you could deal with a potential pitfall can allow you to feel more in control and less worried about anything going wrong.

Let's look at a specific example from my wedding.

Doom List problem – Food supplier not turning up.
Solution to problem – Arranging alternative food.
Person in Charge – Father of the groom.

During the lead-up we had little communication from our evening food supplier, a pizza company. They had reconfirmed they were attending via email, but we were worried they might not show up as we hadn't really had any communication over the phone and we'd never met them before. We were also worried they might not be able to find the venue, and we knew we wouldn't have mobile signal at the reception.

We noted this as an issue on our Doom List. We brainstormed as many solutions to this problem as we could. We settled with a 'Plan B' and wrote the details of this on our Doom List document. We decided if the pizza van didn't attend, or cancelled last minute for whatever reason, we would order twenty pizzas from the local Dominos. We nominated someone from our wedding who wouldn't mind going to collect them, and we'd already prepared 'emergency cash' and given it to the father of the groom for safekeeping.

It sounds really simple, and while it wasn't what we would have wanted for our wedding day, it would have been fine. It would have been a great solution. Our guests would have been fed and there would have been very little fuss. We wouldn't have lost money either, as if the pizza company hadn't turned up, we should have been able to get our money back from our wedding insurance provider.

Thankfully this Plan B didn't happen. But, for the sake of ten minutes' planning, it took away one more worry.

What's worse?

Having takeaway pizza for your evening meal? Or spending your wedding day sobbing because your caterer didn't show up and everyone's gone home hungry while your groom is stuck making fruitless calls to the supplier?

Be prepared for the worst-case scenario. If it does happen, it doesn't matter because you had a backup plan in place. You can enjoy the day for what it is, and then claim off your insurance for any suppliers that might have let you down.

Another bride I worked with had a photographer contact her two months before the wedding to cancel, whilst the bride was disappointed, she had a list of 'reserve' suppliers that she could call on. They were suppliers she'd found as part of her research and they were the people she'd 'almost' booked. Luckily, she could contact the next photographer on her list and confirm the booking. The extra research paid off. She didn't need to 'panic buy' or 'panic choose' a supplier, she could be confident in her back up choice. Of course, everyone wants your day to go to plan, but having a back up plan can save a lot of stress.

Activity Fourteen

THE DOOM LIST

Create your own Doom List. Take some time to think of problems and solutions for your wedding.

Try and think of at least two solutions for each possible problem and then start to list the actions you would need to take to put a Plan B in place.

Here are some ideas you might need to add to your Doom List. Please don't worry, the chances of these happening are very slim! With a Doom List you are taking away possible stress and preparing yourself for all eventualities. The Plan B will always be just that, a Plan B (remember, it won't be your first choice, because you will have already planned that). These are the solutions to make the best of a bad situation — if it should arise.

CATERING:

- Your caterer doesn't show up.

Possible Solution: Plan a shopping list for buffet items someone could buy from a supermarket. Look up local food delivery options. You would have time for someone from your wedding party to buy lots of pre-made sandwiches and crisps if you found out there was a problem with your caterer on the morning of your wedding.

CLOTHING:

- Your wedding dress zip breaks.

Possible solution: Have an emergency sewing kit with you on the wedding day. Also double-check all your dress seams when you leave the dress shop after picking up your dress. Numerous times I've sewn wedding dress hems minutes before brides walked down the aisle!

DECORATIONS:

- The flowers don't get delivered.

Possible Solution: Use other decorations you have around for centrepieces or send a groomsman/bridesmaid to a supermarket or local shop on the morning to buy a beautiful bouquet of flowers to walk down the aisle with. You could even buy extra to decorate the venue. Supermarket flowers will still look great and they rarely run out of stock.

TRANSPORT:

- The car breaks down on the way to the church.

Possible Solution: Keep a local taxi company's phone number handy or ask one bridesmaid to forego the pre-wedding fizz in case they need to drive!

OTHER:

- The photographer calls in sick.

Possible Solution: Allocate a friend in advance who could be a backup photographer. Make sure they bring a camera with them on the day and that they have a copy of the list of photographs you want.

- It rains.

Possible Solution: Buy a beautiful umbrella and a pair of brand-new wellies. Look up some beautiful rainy wedding day pictures on Pinterest and have fun with some creative photography.

- The band doesn't turn up or cancel the day before.

Possible Solution: Make some killer playlists on Spotify with all of your favourite songs, including your first dance song. Have some backup speakers ready and don't forget to sign up for the ad free version of the app!

The Doom List forms a huge part of your working document. It's really useful to share it with your suppliers or wedding coordinator, as they might be able to help, and they will know you are prepared.

You might think you don't need to write all the possible problems down, perhaps because they seem so simple or obvious now. However, when your adrenaline is pumping or a bridesmaid wants to deal with a problem instead of passing it on to the bride or groom, your list of solutions will come in really handy and your friends and suppliers can go straight to your Plan B without having to worry you.

Unplanned problems can be scary. Yet, 99.9 times out of 100 you won't need your backup plans, and everything will work out perfectly. But, for the sake of having a few more documents, a few more plans and some extra ideas, you'll enjoy your wedding day so much more! You will feel more in control and prepared.

Just to stress, these things are extremely unlikely to happen, but it's good to prepare for every eventuality. It acts as a really good fail-safe too, ensuring you are really planning a wedding you care about.

Sometimes the solutions might actually be the responsibility of your venue or your supplier to fix and take control of. However, your worst-case scenario might end up as a list of sensible questions to ask your caterer. For example, what would they do if they electricity went out? Or how would they rearrange the order of the day if they were late? See what their solutions would be, just to check they have thought about it too.

TWENTY

Dealing With Difficult People

When planning your wedding, it is so important that you surround yourself with the right people, the people who will support you and your ideas no matter how crazy or unique they might seem. Surround yourself with the people who will stay up till midnight making DIY decorations with you. Surround yourself with the people who will move heaven and earth to make this day exactly what you want it to be.

Sometimes weddings drive people crazy, but really, it's just because they create a lot of emotion. It's important you know how to deal with all of these emotions that might crop up when you start wedding planning.

There is no such thing as a Bridezilla. A stressed out bride or groom is more often than not caused by someone else. Other people cause stress and chaos. If anyone calls you a Bridezilla or a Groomzilla, that's their problem, not yours.

Are they the sort of people you want to surround yourself with?

I think Bridezilla or Groomzilla are really derogatory terms that seem to have stuck. I don't think it's cool to bounce these words around, even as a joke. When getting married, a couple is making a huge commitment. It's emotional and stressful and when you add the financial commitments you can see why situations can become intense. This is why you need to surround yourself with people who will support you and not cause more work or stress.

Your mother-in-law may have high expectations for how the wedding should look, or your bridesmaids may expect everything to be paid for. Your mum might have lost the plot and demand you have a string quartet. Weddings are full of emotion. People are heavily invested in them personally, emotionally and often financially. This charges the situation and it can get tricky.

Weddings should be full of emotion. But the people you surround yourself with shouldn't add to your stress, no matter how well-meaning their help might be.

The five people you surround yourself with

Did you know you are the culmination of the five people who you spend the most of your time with[1]? Crazy, right? Jim Rohn, the American business philosopher, talks about this. It's terrifying and exciting in equal measure to think you are the sum of your friends. Think about that. Is that who you want to become? The people you surround yourself with make all the difference. But it is so important that you surround yourself with the *right* people.

There are some practical things you can do to ensure you surround yourself with the right people when planning your wedding. And if you are around difficult people, there are some practical tasks you can complete to ensure you have armed yourself with some tools to deal with them.

How to deal with difficult people

- **Boundaries.**

Set really clear boundaries. You don't have to share everything about your wedding planning with everyone. If that nosey so-and-so from work keeps asking you how your plans are going and it's stressing you out talking about it, don't. Set a clear boundary with her and say you don't wish to talk about this at work.

If your sister is pushing to help plan, tell her you appreciate her help, but you only need her ideas on a specific element.

You need to protect yourself by setting boundaries. Your wedding is not always other people's business. Don't shy away from taking control of who you want to share the details of your special day with.

- **Buddy System.**

If you have someone in your family who can't handle your style of wedding, don't meet with them alone. Make sure your partner is with you and make sure your partner backs you up if you face difficult conversations. Most family members will come around to your way of thinking when they realise how much thought you've put into why you want to create your wedding your way.

If you've had to have your second cousin as a bridesmaid but she drives you crazy, don't hang out with her on your own. Make sure you've got the backup of other bridesmaids. The same goes for the big day; if there are certain family members that have a sour face, don't spend time with them, say hello with a bridesmaid in tow and move on.

- **Remember why you started.**

Remember the wedding is about the marriage.

Difficult people will try and pull you into their wedding problems. They might be having a moan or a panic because they don't know where to park on your wedding day. They might ask you for the wedding venue postcode on the evening of your wedding. They might let you know you've inconvenienced them by getting married on a Saturday, and they might have told you 'they've had to use a day of annual leave' three times!

Often people will try and pull you into their stress and worry, but just remember why you started and what your wedding is about – deciding to spend the rest of your life with someone. If other people want to get stressed, let them. This is your day and you're doing it your way. Try and ignore the worries of others.

- **Just say no.**

If you don't want to do anything, don't do it. I'm serious. If your photographer is trying to make you take part in awkward photographs and you don't want to, just say no.

If your bridesmaids want someone to do body shots out of your belly button in Ibiza on your hen party, and you don't want to, *just say no*. If you don't like the hand-me-down veil that your nan wore on her wedding day, don't wear it. This is one of the few times in your life where you get to decide everything, and you get to say no with absolutely no justification.

There is no shame in asking for what you want. Don't worry about setting your boundaries, even if it means disappointing someone else. In ten years' time you'll be more disappointed by missing out on the wedding of your dreams rather than pleasing your mother-in-law by getting married in their garden. This is your day. Surround yourself with people who want to make it special.

Activity Fifteen

WHAT ARE YOU WORRIED ABOUT?

Take some time away from everyone and write down some of the people and the elements that are worrying you about your day.

Ask yourself:

- Which people do you worry about?
- What are you afraid of happening?
- What can you do about it?
- Who can help you?
- Who do you want to surround yourself with?
- What do you love about them?
- How can they help?

It's important to think about some of the strategies you could put into place to deal with people and situations you are worried about. Don't forget to talk to your partner too, let them know your concerns. List solutions for your worries or concerns and start acting on them. You don't want to be worrying on your wedding day. If you can act now, you should.

Often friends and family are just trying to help, they might not realise they are causing worry. Can you start a conversation with someone today and let them know how you feel?

TWENTY-ONE

Being Present

The one thing you'll hear time and time again from people who are married:

"It all goes too fast."

Not just the day itself, but all the preparation and the lead-up to the wedding too. If it all goes to plan, you only do this once, and if you are on your second or third wedding, you won't have another one like *this* one, with *these* people at *this* moment in time.

It is so important that you are present and soak up everything, the whole lead-up, and enjoy it. Enjoy seeing your friends getting excited, enjoy seeing your family being a part of this, enjoy seeing something that you have built come to life.

The biggest mistake people make is that they try to do too much, and this distracts them. For all my brides, I'll take pictures of the final setup on the morning of their wedding and then share them as they get their make-up done or their hair finalised. I'll answer any questions and reply to the reels of checks and worries with a nod. It's all been sorted. There is nothing left for them to do. It's time now to get married.

A recent article from *The Independent* found 52% of British brides declared the whole wedding planning process as "stressful"[1]. This makes me so sad; please don't let your wedding be stressful, let it be fun! Let yourself see your wedding vision statement come true and enjoy it.

The best way to be present on your wedding day

1. Take time and talk to yourself!

Take some time as you move through the wedding day, even if it's five minutes, and have a little word with yourself. Remind yourself, this is it! This is your wedding day. Soak it up! Say it out loud. "This is my wedding day." It helps your brain record the moment and it helps you stop and *live* in the moment too.

2. Have a wedding mantra.

Have a wedding day mantra. I know this can sound silly. I used to think mantras were silly too, but then in the lead-up to your wedding day you might face so many worries and negative thoughts that are simply untrue. You've done the work, the plans are in place, just change the narrative of the words that are in your head.

Create a mantra that you can repeat to yourself.

For example:

> "*I will feel full of energy on my wedding day. I will look beautiful and everyone will have a good time.*"

Repeating this can help you to calm down. It can help you focus on the elements you can control. It sounds so self-indulgent, but it should be; mantras are for you alone, for your self-belief and self-esteem. Replace any negative thoughts in your head with positive ones.

3. Focus on what you are looking forward to.

Obviously, you are going to be looking forward to the whole wedding, but really think about the specific parts you are looking forward to the most. Is it walking into the reception room knowing all your friends and family are there? Walking down the aisle? The food? Seeing your partner? Then when these parts happen, take them in fully. Say to yourself:

> "This is the bit you were looking forward to, and you're in it *now*."

Try and narrow down some of the parts you are really looking forward to and when they happen take a mental snapshot.

4. Delegate!

This is the most important thing you need to do to allow yourself to enjoy your wedding day and be present. You need to delegate.

As an on-the-day wedding coordinator, I can talk about the advantages of hiring someone to take the lead on your wedding day, but even if you don't want to pay and hire someone, you need to delegate your working document and your wedding plans to someone you love and trust. A bridesmaid, a groomsman or best friend. They need to run the show so you can enjoy your day. Who can you ask for support with this?

You don't want to be on the phone to a wedding supplier, you want to be dancing on tables and sipping champagne. Give your wedding to someone else and let them take charge. You've done the work, so it's time you enjoyed it. This will help you be present in the actual event rather than trying to manage it.

Activity Sixteen

YOUR WEDDING DAY MANTRA

Take some time to create a wedding day mantra. This is different to your wedding vision statement, although it might have some similar elements. This mantra needs to be all about you.

Think about what you want circling through your head on your wedding day. Repeating these words can help with mindfulness and can reduce stress. By repeating the same phrase, it can help you relax. Training your mind to focus on positive and healthy words and thoughts that you want to bring into fruition.

Write your wedding mantra on a small card, carry it in with you and memorise it by heart. On the day of your wedding keep repeating it until you forget to, because you're so present in your wedding day!

TWENTY-TWO

All That Matters is Marriage

Your wedding day is a choice.

When you wake up on your wedding day, you have a choice. You can roll with the punches and embrace the love of the people you've chosen to surround yourself with. Or you can worry that the flowers aren't quite the shade you ordered, the centrepieces aren't quite central, and the food was a bit cold. You only get this day once, and if you choose to look at it with joy and perfection, that's how it will be and that's how you'll remember it.

Choose to let go. Choose to enjoy it all. Whatever happens. If you do, it will be the best day of your life. You will feel how you had hoped, and your guests will too.

My wedding day choice, a personal story:

Blinking my eyes open slowly, the daylight streamed through the blinds. It was morning. The day I'd been planning and dreaming about for so long was finally here.

I hadn't slept.

The tower clock on the village school chimed every hour on the hour throughout the night. I'd heard it every hour, apart from 2am and 4am. But I didn't care. Two hours of sleep and I felt awake and full of energy. A smile pulled at my lips and stretched to my cheeks.

I'd decided to sleep away from my bridesmaids on my own, and I was grateful for a few moments of peace and quiet. Throwing the duvet off, I padded my way across to the window. I took a deep breath and lifted the blind.

Grey drizzle.

I smiled even harder. I truly didn't care. I had decided to let everything go. On this day I was going to be the most relaxed version of myself. Whatever happened, it would all be okay, because I was getting married to my best friend, the person I wanted to spend the rest of my life with.

Rain, shine or showers, I was letting everything go on my wedding day. I knew I'd planned everything to the best of my ability. It wasn't in my hands anymore. I just needed to enjoy my day for what it was, whatever that would be, because I would never get it again.

I dropped the blind and reminded myself I wasn't in control of anything but my attitude and my determination to be present and peaceful for my whole wedding day.

I repeated my wedding day mantra, took a deep breath, and walked downstairs, knowing the day was going to be perfect.

By the time I walked out of the church, the sun was so warm and bright it covered the village in a crisp shade of golden sunlight

My advice to you, smile even if it rains. Choose to embrace your wedding day, whatever happens. As long as you get married, that's all that matters.

Part Four Summary

Whilst you don't want to fixate on what could go wrong, it's worth exploring the potential pitfalls so you can be prepared and present on your wedding day.

To sum up, in this section:

- You should have created your very own Doom List, looking at all of the things that could go wrong, so you can be prepared and nip any problems in the bud.
- You should have started to reflect on your wedding as whole. You've got your wedding timeline and task list to work through, but you should be able to see the big picture and all of the bite-sized tasks that need to be completed to make up that big picture.
- You should have started to set clear boundaries for how to deal with the people around you.
- You should have made plans and reflected on how you can be more present on your wedding day.

We started with the big picture, your overall vision of your DIY wedding. Then you created your vision statement, your neon shining light that has been guiding you through the whole process. We started with your why, the reasoning and the sparkling passion and feeling behind your wedding.

Then we moved in, we narrowed it down slightly, moving on to your starting place on the map. We looked at how you would research and plan, exploring to what extent you wanted to let your wedding become 'DIY'. Then we looked at creating a scaffolding to hang all your plans on – the wedding planning timeline and your working document.

We looked at every single element of your wedding and you examined it in even more detail. Listing, brainstorming, breaking elements down to build them up again. We also looked at what might happen if things go wrong. You fixed it. You created a plan B.

And now what, what next?

You've planned the best day of your life. It made you feel exactly like you wanted to feel and you'll remember that feeling forever, you'll hold onto it and you'll move into your happily ever after.

Part Five – The Happily Ever After

TWENTY-THREE

The Cleanup

You're married, *now what?* In this section we will look at the often-forgotten elements that make a wedding, the clearing down, tidying up and the taboo of the wedding blues.

What happens when your dreams come true?

I've seen so many couples get stressed with the wedding cleanup, pressured by venues or suppliers to "hurry up" and get out by the required time or face charges. That's the last thing you need the day after your wedding.

You've been organised and you've planned in the whole lead-up, so why wouldn't you plan the last little hurdle? Think about how you would want the cleanup to feel.

Yeah, feelings again.

Depending on your venue, you might have to clean up on the actual wedding day, and this is where you must have a plan for delegation. If you can, push for the cleanup to take place the day after.

It can feel so sad walking into your venue when it's all over, but planning for the cleanup is just as important as planning the setup. You don't want to end on a bad note, or with chaos. You want to plan the tidying up and closedown carefully, so wedding items won't get lost or broken and you can get back to celebrating.

You're not going to want to do it, but it can be fun too.

How to plan for the post-wedding cleanup

- List all of the jobs that need completing in painstaking detail. List them so clearly someone else could complete them.
- Allocate one person to collect and keep safe all the valuable items (wedding cards and gifts) and all of the sentimental items you might want to keep (table settings, your bouquet, seating plans etc.).
- Delegate and clarify who is doing what. Write this out and let the person know.
- Reward your helpers. Why not plan for food or drinks afterwards? Think about how you can make the cleanup fun. Make sure they feel valued and appreciated.
- Check your contracts and the return details of your hired items. They might have to been cleaned or left in a certain place. Check these well before your wedding day and have a plan in place.
- Check all of your suppliers, and the venue, have be paid. More often than not you will have had to do this before the wedding day. But sometimes bands and DJs might request cash on the night or the day after.
- Check you receive security deposits back for any

hire items. Task someone to take pictures so there can be no confusion over damaged or broken items.

- The same goes for your venue. Double-check and take pictures of how you've left the venue, just in case any problems or questions arise.
- Take pictures. Not just of hire items and the venue, but of all your friends and family helping you clean up. This is just as much a part of your DIY wedding as the setup.
- Enjoy it. Play music. Enjoy a glass of fizz.
- Try not to waste anything — food, flowers, drinks. Have you got a plan for who will put away any leftover food in the evening? A few minutes of wrapping and saving will mean a feast the next day. What about your flowers? Could you arrange to leave them at the church or venue? Or can you give them away to your guests as they leave?
- Moving cards and gifts from the venue straight after the wedding has finished is the best option. Why not ask a bridesmaid or a groomsman to look after this task?

Saying thank you

It's also really important that you thank people who have helped you. And, if for some reason the wedding day did 'go wrong' or you had to use some of the solutions on your Doom List, focus on the *good*. You got married! That was the goal. The most important thing. You still need to thank people for everything they've done. Ending your wedding on a 'thank you' will leave you feeling grateful and joyful.

When you leave your bare tent, tipi, marquee, hall, or reception room it will feel strange, the start of a goodbye. No more wedding planning or DIY crafting. But it will also be the start of a new adventure.

Marriage.

TWENTY-FOUR

Wedding Blues

A lot of people don't talk about this, but I want to touch on this topic because you need to be prepared. The wedding blues might float past you as you start your honeymoon period of marriage. Or they might whack you round the face as the wheels of your return honeymoon flight lands with a bumpy thud. Either way, forewarned is forearmed.

I don't get to see many of my brides after they are married and into their happily ever after, so I think it's good that we talk about this now.

After your wedding you will be on such a high, so happy and in awe of what you created. And then some time will pass, and this amount of time is different for everyone, and you'll start to wonder what you did before your wedding. You'll feel like something is missing and you won't know what to do with your time.

Part of this is also because you were *literally* a different person before you got married. You were a Miss or a Mr. You were not a husband or wife. So much will have changed, yet at the same time everything might be feeling exactly as it did. Change and normal will mix and twist with expectation and confusion.

Planning and making decisions and DIY-ing gave you a focus and a goal. It might be that you need another goal and something else to work towards. Or it could be a great time to find a new hobby. You've managed to add wedding planning to a busy schedule, so why not take up something new instead of filling the time with TV? Or it might be the perfect opportunity for you to rest and have some time not doing anything.

The wedding blues can often creep up and hide themselves in loneliness. When planning a wedding we wouldn't think twice about messaging a friend with an idea or tagging someone in a beautiful dress or wedding suggestion on Facebook, or screenshotting pins and keeping cutouts from magazines, but after the wedding, it feels like there is less of a reason to reach out to a friend. With no set purpose to the contact, your relationships can drift. And this is where the wedding blues can kick the hardest, turning from the palest of blues to a deep, dark navy.

My wedding blues, a personal story:

The sun dripped through the umbrella and warmed my toes as I lay on the soft lounger. The waves crashing on the reef out towards the horizon sounded like a recording, perfectly timed and pitched at exactly the right volume. The sky was as blue as the sea and yet crystal-clear. They danced together, merging to create a picture-perfect view.

Yes, the Maldives is every bit as beautiful as you can imagine.

The only place in the world that really looks like the pictures. No filter needed for our honeymoon destination. I sipped on my ice cold can of Coke. As the beads of condensation dropped on my lap, in between the sound of the bubbles fizzing from the can and over the noise of the breaking waves, I could hear a nagging voice. Quiet at first, but the more I listened the louder it got. It whispered initially:

What now?

And then as more days and weeks elapsed between the wedding and the happily ever after, it started to shout.

What now?

You see, the wedding planning had been everything I'd hoped. All consuming, de-stressing, mind-filling, soul-filling happiness.

But now what?

I'd be married and have a lifetime of adventures, of course, but what was I going to do on a rainy Sunday afternoon? Or on a Wednesday evening after work? How would I fill those Saturdays I'd spent making and DIY-ing? Scouring second-hand shops for ideas, flicking through bridal magazines in cafes? What about the WhatsApp group I had with the bridesmaids?

What now?

How to manage the wedding blues

- **Start making something else.** You could make a really cute wedding scrapbook with examples of all the elements you've made for your wedding. Keeping busy is a great way to distract yourself and use all of those DIY skills you've been developing.
- **Don't forget the thank you cards.** When we express gratitude, it can allow us to feel more thankful and happy. Spending a lot of time writing long, personal and meaningful thank you cards for the guests that attended and helped with your DIY wedding can be a really great way to deal with the wedding blues.
- **Enjoy looking over your wedding photos and reminiscing.** Give yourself permission to feel this way; don't feel embarrassed or shameful. Your feelings are perfectly legitimate. Your wedding day was amazing! Take time to look at the pictures, share stories and laugh at the good times.
- **Plan some dates and events to look forward to.** Your wedding day was a huge thing to look forward to, so why not add some other events to your calendar. Holidays you could save for? Or weekly walks and pub lunches with friends?
- **Talk about your feelings.** This might seem really obvious, but so many people struggle to talk about how they really feel. If you feel like you might be hit with the wedding blues, don't wait until after the wedding. Start talking to your

friends about it now, so they can be ready to support you. If you do feel like you are getting really low, make sure you talk to your doctor or health professional too.

If you don't have these feelings, that's perfectly valid too. There isn't a right or wrong way to feel. It's just good to talk about it. You might be relieved. You might throw that glue gun away, thankful you never have to look at it again!

And remember, it's just the beginning. This is the start of something new and that can be exciting too.

Activity Seventeen

THE MARRIAGE BUCKET LIST

It's time to write a marriage bucket list!

This should be a fun activity, not something to be rushed. Why not go out for the day, or plan a special evening at home just to work on this activity?

List all the things you want to do together as a married couple:

- Starting new traditions.
- Places you want to go.
- Goals you want to achieve.
- Ideas, dreams, thoughts and plans.
- Celebrating wedding anniversaries in a certain way.

Have fun and think of some crazy ideas you'd like to work towards as you start out in married life. Make sure you write them all down and save them somewhere that you can access easily. Each year on your wedding anniversary, why not look at the list and add to it?

TWENTY-FIVE

Documenting Your Day

At first, your wedding day will be so clear in your head. The DIY details you spent weeks making will glow as you think of how they looked on display. The exact colours of the flowers in your bouquet. The smells. The food. You think you'll remember that delicious taste of the first bite of your cake forever. Everything will seem like a picture-perfect memory. And it will be for a few weeks, months even. But eventually the picture will start to fade.

The good news is you are in control of this. You can write everything down; you can document your day and seal the memories forever. The details can be saved.

The lesson I learnt the hard way, a personal story:

I was walking with a friend when she turned and asked:

"What about you? What was your something old, something new, something borrowed and something blue?"

I felt myself stop moving, sucking in air with a sudden gasp. I couldn't remember. A simple question. But I didn't know the answer.

Shaking my head, I tried to pull the memory back from the dusty depths of my brain. I closed my eyes. How could I forget?

Fuzzy images started to form. I remembered half of a moment, fragments of a memory. My bridesmaids had sorted my something old, new, borrowed and blue. I can see it now — they gave them to me as gifts the night before my wedding. But what were they? I desperately tried to grasp on to the flickering answers as they danced across my thoughts.

I thought I would remember this forever. I didn't think I'd ever forget.

That's the problem. We don't think we will forget. After spending years of planning, surrounded by the details, we think we will remember them forever. But we don't. Unless we write it down.

This is why you've worked so hard on creating a *feeling* for your wedding, because feelings are a lot harder to forget. But the details still need to be written down to cement them into your memory bank. You need to save your wedding story.

How to save your memories

This is why I now recommend to all my couples that they write down the details of their wedding day, as soon as they can. It is so important that you write it all down. Even if it's a few scribbles, get it down whilst the happy memories are still fresh.

This could be in the form of a diary entry or thoughts in a private notebook. Even something as simple as a quick note of what happened and when will be a great thing to look back on in one, ten and twenty years' time. It will be worth it.

How you can document your wedding day:

- **Create a wedding photo book** — This could be ordered from your photographer or you could use an online service like Photobox. They often have discounts and offers. Make a night of it when you make your photo book. Put your wedding songs on, have some nice drinks and have fun reliving your favourite wedding moments.
- **Create a handmade wedding scrapbook** — Order your own printed out photos and add comments and stories to the pictures. Stick in the order of service and even examples of your wedding invites. Why not get friends to add their stories too? This scrapbook isn't meant to look perfect; it's meant to capture your wedding day and document it as it happened. There are lots of lovely scrapbooks you can buy. Why not have one on display on your coffee table or bookshelf? Friends will love to look back at the memories.
- **Create a keepsake box** — Keep copies of all the items that relate to your wedding. Copies of invites or RSVPs, wedding cards, table settings or even favours (if you can). Place all these items into a nicely decorated box. It will be a living example

of some of the wonderful items you created and the ideas you had for your wedding.

- **Turn your wedding day cards into a creative scrapbook** — In years to come it will be lovely to look back and see all of the kind words family and friends shared with you on your wedding day.

- **Create a wedding picture display in a box frame** — Don't let your DIY skills stop after your wedding! Why not buy a box frame (sometimes called a shadow frame) and display pictures and items from the wedding, like cards and invites with the lyrics of your first dance song? Or press flowers from your bouquet? It will be a great talking point when people see it.

- **Get your wedding dress framed** — A statement decoration and memory that you could look at every day in your house.

- **Make your own wedding video** — Videographers can be expensive, so why not have a go at making your own wedding video with clips from friends? It doesn't have to be perfect, because you don't have to show anyone. It can be just for you and your partner.

- **Write a letter to your partner about the wedding day** — This version of the day will be from y*our* point of view and it will be a lovely present for your partner to open and cherish. It will also be a good way for you to reflect on your wedding day.

- **Make an album on Facebook with all your wedding pictures** — You'll get a reminder each year as the pictures show up on your Facebook memories.

- **Keep some decorations from the day** —
  Use them to decorate your house. This is a great
  way to reuse wedding items and get value for
  money from items you might have bought for the
  wedding.
- **Write the story of your wedding day** —
  This could be as a book and you could even self-
  publish it, so you can get a printed copy to keep
  forever.

Top Tip — Don't forget to add some of these extra post-
wedding costs into your budget. After your wedding it
might be difficult to find some spare cash to pay for them.
You'll be glad you budgeted some money to finish off your
wedding day by documenting it.

Part Five Summary

You'll experience a rollercoaster of emotions as you start to close the wedding magazines and Pinterest boards, but the end of your wedding should feel like a huge accomplishment, the culmination of your hard work, dedication and creativity — the joining of two lives. You'll have lots to remember and celebrate and, what's more, you'll be married.

In this section we have explored:

- How you can document and capture your wedding day, making sure you are saving the best moments for years to come.
- How to plan the cleanup and shutdown after your wedding, ensuring you've got a clear plan so you can delegate if you need to.
- You'll know what to do if you experience some of the more painful emotions that can appear after your wedding, and you'll be armed with an amazing married life bucket list.

The End

You've done it. You've planned the wedding of your dreams. And what's more, you've planned a wedding that *feels* amazing and doesn't just *look* amazing. In doing this, you've made your wedding unique and completely different to every other wedding on Pinterest.

Together through this book we have explored:

- Wedding feelings and priorities — ensuring that your wedding day is a reflection of your values and wishes.
- Wedding planning timelines, budgets and how to find the best suppliers based on your wedding priorities.
- You've made plans and know what to do if it all goes wrong.
- You've worked on homework tasks and activities, designing your wedding with less stress and more creativity.

- You've set boundaries and surrounded yourself with people who want the best for you.
- You know how to document and record your wedding so you can remember it forever.

I hope you've had fun and I hope your wedding day is memorable and meaningful.

Your Task List

Below is an overview of all the activities mentioned in the book. If you haven't already, get started on these activities and start planning your wedding. Have fun!

- **Activity One: Love Letters**. Write a love letter to your partner. Let them know what you are looking forward to the *most* about getting married.
- **Activity Two: What Does DIY Mean to You?** Spend some time talking about why you have chosen to go down the DIY route. Think about the elements you really want to DIY, make a list of them and why.
- **Activity Three**: **What Feelings Do You Want?** Write down some of the key 'feelings' you would like to have in all of the different parts of your wedding day. Get clear on how you would like your wedding day to feel.
- **Activity Four: Your Wedding Goals**. Set goals that relate to the feelings you want to create and experience on your wedding day. This will help

you refine your goals and make them clearer as you go through the planning stages.

- **Activity Five: Tell Me What You Really _Really_ Want?** Narrow down your five top wedding priorities. It doesn't matter what your priorities are, as long as you know they are what matter to _you._

- **Activity Six: Wedding Vision Statement.** Create your wedding vision statement with your partner. Add up the reasons why you want to get married, with the overarching feelings goals you've set and then add the wedding elements that are your priorities. Let this be your guide.

- **Activity Seven: Part One Homework.** Design your wedding mood board, capturing the feelings, vision statement and priorities in a visual form.

- **Activity Eight: Where Are You Starting?** For this task you will be determining your wedding driver, the primary pillar that's leading your decision making. Answer the questions to try and assess which wedding pillar is your driver.

- **Activity Nine: Your Wedding Timeline.** Map out your wedding planning timeline using the standard task list. Make sure you make the timeline personal to your priorities.

- **Activity Ten: Extra Timeline Details.** For this activity you will need to go back through the personal wedding planning timeline you created in the last activity, and then add all _additional things_ you want to do under each month.

- **Activity Eleven: Part Two Homework.** Confirm your wedding planning timeline, add lots of the extra fun elements, but also make sure you know where the pressure points are. Start to list how you can deal with those pressures. Print your timeline off and stick it somewhere you'll see it every day in your house.

- **Activity Twelve: The Budget.** Go through each item on the budget list and estimate (roughly) the amount of money or the percentage of your budget that you would like to allocate to each area. Start to plan out what your limits are.

- **Activity Thirteen: Part Three Homework.** Map out your dream wedding day timeline.

- **Activity Fourteen: The Doom List.** Take some time to think of problems and solutions you could examine and add to your own Doom List. Try and think of at least two solutions for each possible problem and then start to list the actions you would need to take to put a plan B in place.

- **Activity Fifteen: What Are You Worried About?** Take some time away from everyone and write down some of the people and the elements you are worried about and brainstorm solutions.

- **Activity Sixteen: Your Wedding Day Mantra.** Take some time to create a wedding day mantra. This is different to your wedding vision statement, although it might have some similar elements. This mantra needs to be all about you.

- **Activity Seventeen: The Marriage Bucket List.** Write a marriage bucket list!

Your Free Gift & The Next Steps

Thank you for reading this book. I hope it helps you plan a DIY wedding that *feels* like you. If you've enjoyed reading this book, please leave an honest review.

Your gift

To receive free downloadable worksheets to support you through the activities in this book, head over to www.peakdistrictevents.com and join the mailing list.

You can find more DIY weddings tips at www.peakdistrictevents.com. I also advertise wedding workshops and full days of wedding planning support and advice to ensure your wedding runs problem-free!

Get in touch

I can't wait to hear all about your wedding. I love to see pictures, but mostly importantly I love to hear all about how your wedding felt. You can get in touch: Laura@peakdistrictevents.com

About the Author

Laura is the owner of Peak District Events, an event management company based in the Peak District, Derbyshire.

Laura specialises in DIY wedding coordination, helping brides and grooms bring their ideas to life but letting them get all the credit and all the joy.

Laura has a degree in event management, but more importantly, years and years of experience working in and on events, especially weddings. And this is where she can help you. In this book and through her wedding coordination she shares her knowledge, industry secrets and experience to ensure you bring your dream wedding to life.

You can find out more about Laura and her wedding planning services at www.peakdistrictevents.com.

References

4. Feelings Matter

1. Emotional Memory – We remember events for longer when emotions are attached to them. https://www.memory-key.com/memory/emotion

5. Goals. Goals. Goals.

1. Manifesting Defintion. https://gabbybernstein.com/dos-donts-manifesting

10. What Next?

1. Parkinson's Law – *"Work expands so as to fill the time available for its completion."*
   https://www.economist.com/news/1955/11/19/parkinsons-law
2. The average wedding takes 528 hours to plan. https://www.independent.co.uk/life-style/dating/wedding-planning-time-venue-dress-food-price-engagement-a8788076.html

14. Let's Talk Money

1. A recent Hitched.co.uk article found the average cost of a wedding in the UK (in 2019) was an eye-watering £31,974. https://www.hitched.co.uk/wedding-planning/organising-and-planning/the-average-wedding-cost-in-the-uk-revealed/

20. Dealing With Difficult People

1. You are the culmination of the five people who you spend the most of your time with. https://www.businessinsider.com/jim-rohn-youre-the-average-of-the-five-people-you-spend-the-most-time-with-2012-7?r=US&IR=T

21. Being Present

1. 52% of British brides declared the whole wedding planning process as "stressful". https://www.independent.co.uk/life-style/wedding-planning-stress-british-people-study-uk-a8776041.html

Printed in Great Britain
by Amazon

79939636R00132